The Tao of Tarot

The Way to Health, Happiness and Illumination through Qigong Dreaming

First published by O Books, 2010
O Books is an imprint of John Hunt Publishing Ltd., The Bothy, Deershot Lodge, Park Lane, Ropley, Hants, SO24 0BE, UK
office1@o-books.net
www.o-books.net

Distribution in:

UK and Europe
Orca Book Services
orders@orcabookservices.co.uk
Tel: 01202 665432 Fax: 01202 666219
Int. code (44)

USA and Canada
NBN
custserv@nbnbooks.com
Tel: 1 800 462 6420 Fax: 1 800 338 4550

Australia and New Zealand
Brumby Books
sales@brumbybooks.com.au
Tel: 61 3 9761 5535 Fax: 61 3 9761 7095

Far East (offices in Singapore, Thailand, Hong Kong, Taiwan)
Pansing Distribution Pte Ltd
kemal@pansing.com
Tel: 65 6319 9939 Fax: 65 6462 5761

South Africa
Alternative Books
altbook@peterhyde.co.za
Tel: 021 555 4027 Fax: 021 447 1430

Design: Stuart Davies

ISBN: 978 1 84694 265 5

A CIP catalogue record for this book is available from the British Library.

Printed by Digital Book Print

The Tao of Tarot

The Way to Health, Happiness and Illumination through Qigong Dreaming

Christina Bjergo

Winchester, UK
Washington, USA

CONTENTS

Dedication

To my beloved mother for encouraging me to teach, write and follow my dreams.

Acknowledgements

Deepest thanks and appreciation to:

My dad who always told me I could.

My grandparents whose lives continue to inspire me.

My husband Karl for the continued love, loyalty, and support.

My children Alie and Nick, my biggest blessing and greatest gift to the world.

My Qigong teachers, Professor Chen, Teri Applegate, Liu He and Liz Bolza.

My Qigong mentor, Roger Lore, who showed by example how to live Qigong.

My friend and fellow author, Karen Tate, for the fun-filled journey through Turkey and your compassionate efforts to help a fledgling writer like myself.

My wonderful guides to ancient wisdom traditions around the world, Mark Amaru-Pinkham and Andrea Mikana-Pinkham with Sacred Sites Journeys.

Thanks for the Hill of Tara and the Chalice Well photos Andrea.

My publisher, O Books, for their down to earth efficiency and publication of this book.

My editor, Jill Kelly, for improving my punctuation and stretching me to grow as a writer.

My buddy, Kristian Vockler, for promoting Qigong and sharing the blog.

All my wonderful family, friends, students and clients who have touched my life and taught me along the journey.

August Moon, Village Pearl and the Unitarian Universality Fellowship in Vancouver for providing free space for the community to practice Qigong.

The Dreamtime and the spiritual guidance that unites us all.

Introduction

Tarot cards are thought to have originated in the early 1400's in Italy. They became increasingly widespread in the English speaking world with Rider's publication of the Waite tarot in 1909. Designed under the instruction of A. E. Waite, an author of magic, divination and alchemy who was a member of the Hermetic Order of the Golden Dawn, the Waite cards are known for their sacred universal symbolism. They are commonly used as a form of fortune telling by both self interpreters and professional readers alike. When understood as a wellness and divination tool, however, the major trump cards reorganized also depict 'the Way' to health, happiness and spiritual illumination. The process to achieving these goals is integrally linked with classic spiritual traditions, Chinese medicine and the intuitive faculty of dreaming as will be shown in the pages ahead. Though largely unknown, the tarot contains non-verbal spiritual wisdom inclusive to different beliefs and religions around the world. The illustrations of the cards are divinely encoded. Their symbolic language opens us to inspiration from God.

The sacred images upon the cards become keys that, when unlocked, provide insight into what is working in our lives and what needs to change. Global meanings behind the symbols pictured on the cards offer valuable clues to help the psyche shift consciousness towards greater joy and well being. The individual cards are like snapshots of dreams we might experience in our sleep. Tarot images and dreams ultimately come from Source and may be viewed as one and the same. The tarot as dream teaches about the hidden truth behind our existence. In pondering the archetypal symbolism in the card images, benevolent guidance percolates up into awareness so that important lessons can be interpreted, integrated and appropriately acted upon. The journey to wellness is accessible

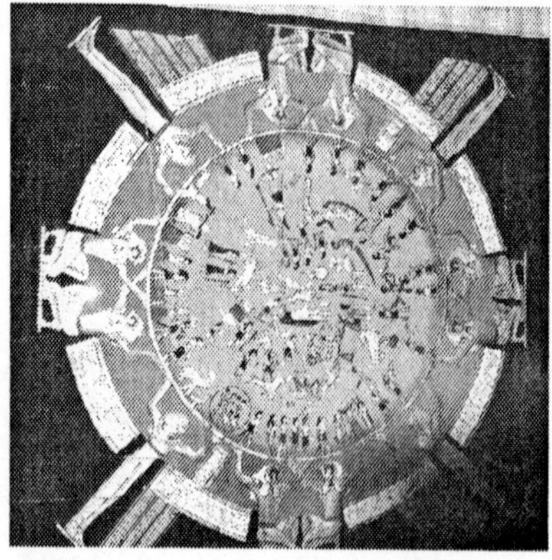

The Astrological Wheel from the Temple of Hathor in Dendera, Egypt shows the cycle of the stars in the sky. Reflecting upon the celestial bodies was a means to bring heaven to earth.

to any of us willing to look at the meaning of dreams and honestly see what the visual mirror reflects about ourselves.

The word *tarot* is derived from 'rota' meaning 'revolving wheel' and 'tota' meaning 'total'.[1] Each card in a deck represents a movement or position of the wheel. The tarot cards offer an inner exploration into the cycles of life and the seasons of the soul. Ultimately, the circular pathway of the tarot journey takes each of us inward to the center of ourselves, to the totality of our being, which is the source of all healing. Within the central hub of the wheel we find spiritual transcendence whatever our faith or creed. The tarot is similar to the astrological wheel of ancient cultures, the Mayan calendar, the Celtic Wheel of the Sun and the teachings of the Native American Medicine Wheel. The tarot pictures create a visual depiction of the Taoist *I Ching*, a guidebook detailing the infinite intelligence, called the Tao, that underlies nature's fluctuations. The idea that

> The ancient Chinese knew how to work internally with the transcendental serpent power called central qi for their physical, emotional and spiritual development. Famed mythologist Joseph Campbell believed that 4,000 year old bronze spiral artifacts from China predate what would later develop into kundalini practices in India.

predictability and constancy underlie life's changes is of primary significance. When understood and followed, the harmonious flow of the t(a)r(o)t leads to individual, family, community and global unity and peace.

The revolving wheel is, in essence, the sacred serpent spiral (spiral), a cross cultural and ageless symbol of spiritual union. The spiral was one of the most sacred symbols of Europe during the Neolithic period.[2] Images of spirals have been found in temples of ancient Egypt and India, on archeological artifacts of early China and on holy megalithic structures of the Americas, Europe and Australia. In the Incan tradition of South America, the sacred spiral represents Pachamama or Mother Nature. The spiral is also the basis of the spiritual-based whirling dervish of Sufi Muslims and the Kabala of mystical Judaism. It continues to be ritualized through Native American ceremonies in the United States, May Pole celebrations throughout Europe and labyrinth walks around the world. In Tantric Hinduism and the Buddhism of Asia, the spiral is synonymous with the potent transformative feminine properties of the kundalini or coiled serpent energy and is a means to spiritual ascension. The spiral is also a symbol of unity in China since ancient times. To Qigong practitioners, the spiral is the whirling void of the life force energy called *qi* that unifies heaven and earth and everything in existence. Working to build and refine *qi* through the body-minded practice of Qigong we access a reality beyond duality, the timeless dimension of our inherent oneness.

> A seven part Peruvian rainbow spiral is an Incan symbol of Pachamama or Mother Nature and represents the divine reflected in the physical world.

The major *arcana* of the tarot are the original 22 picture cards. Arcana is typically defined as secret or hidden knowledge, the secret of nature that traditional alchemists sought and a secret or mysterious remedy or elixir. Hidden to the untrained eye within the cards, particularly the original 22, are secrets to youthfulness, long life and abundance, the goals sought after by alchemists and others of past and present. The alchemical transformation process is depicted in the cards as the Ouroborus: the dragon serpent biting its own tail. The revolving wheel of the Ouroborus is the Wheel of Fortune of the tarot leading us back to our wholeness. This important Taoist symbol represents the cyclical nature of immanent life, the balance of destruction and creation forces leading to transcendence.

Obtaining the elixir of immortality has been the focus of religious seekers since the beginning of human culture. Myths and stories concerning the quest for the Holy Grail and the promise of spiritual enlightenment abound around the world. The mysterious origins of alchemy have their roots in early shamanic cultures, then were recorded and popularized in early Egypt and China. Alchemy later spread through Hellenistic Greece, early Islam and medieval Europe.[3] The alchemical arts influenced Judeo Christian spiritual development and continue in contemporary times. Individuals in search of *gnosis* or self knowledge practice inner alchemy. By removing ignorance and self imposed barriers, known as karma in the East, alchemists ultimately achieve self realization, the ultimate goal of the human soul. To know the self, is in essence to know God.

European alchemy focused on transmuting base metals, such as lead, into gold. As much as a thousand years earlier, however, Chinese Taoist alchemists used inner cultivation techniques of Qigong to find eternal life and restore order to the world around them.[3] Combining body movement, intention, meditation, breath work and sound healing, Qigong practice facilitates the union of intuitive and intellectual faculties. Through this body-oriented exercise from the East, spiritual goals of everlasting life can be obtainable. The Taoist legends of the Eight Immortals show that spiritual rebirth is possible for people of all ages, genders and social status. Historic individuals are known to have achieved immortality and entered the Realm of the Immortals upon death. Alchemical ascension is glimpsed within the Christian Bible as well. Within *Corinthians,* the dead can be made incorruptible and mortals obtain immortality and go to heaven following Jesus' example. Methods for obtaining immortal life may have been suppressed by strict Communist and Orthodox ideologies yet alchemical knowledge survives today.

Taoism as a philosophy is the foundation of contemporary Traditional Chinese Medicine. Likewise, the Asian secrets of health and wellness are weaved within the popular and symbolic images of the famous Waite tarot deck and depicted in nightly dreams. The once dormant body-focused process of alchemical transformation through Qigong is now resurfacing through dreams and other intuitive promptings to help many overcome individual and collective difficulties during this critical period in history. I have seen it repeatedly in my clients, students and those who email queries regarding their dreams. Something is awakening in our collective consciousness.

Psychologist and renowned dream worker Carl Jung believed that the alchemists had discovered the unconscious.[3] Alchemists in general place great importance on dream cultivation as well as the development of intuition. Everything operates by divine order and has underlying meaning. With nothing happening by accident, we exist in a synchronistic dream world, the hidden world of God. Dreaming, whether by day or night, is a means of tapping into this unseen reality. Dreams are written down and analyzed by alchemists for their spiritual insight.[2] Examining the appropriate Chinese Medicine symbolism within the cards adds a critical dimension to the spiritual significance of dreaming as one of the tarot's sacred teachings.

In Part I of this book Lao Tzu's guidance on how to understand 'the Way' is reviewed through discussion of the Fool and Magician cards. Dreams, Lao Tzu wrote in the *Tao De Jing,* are the appearance of the infinite intelligence and help open the doorway to the golden secret of all life. Internal cultivation techniques like Qigong quiet the ego mind and awaken inner awareness helping us mature. Applying the insight found in these two cards we can have unlimited access to knowledge and learn to improve our lives without hardship. The *Tao De Jing*, like recently discovered Christian texts, ultimately teaches that there is no greater teacher than direct spiritual experience.

In Part II, Qigong theory and Asian symbolism found in the tarot are described more fully. The Hermit, the Star, Temperance, the Sun, the Empress and the Emperor together depict the process of practicing Spiral Qigong. (Note: An all in one Spiral Qigong description is also available at the end of the book to facilitate practice of this form.) As a spontaneous movement meditation, Spiral Qigong allows the infinite potential of the universe to direct and move the practitioner. Spiral Qigong helps integrate the conscious with the unconscious mind and is a powerful tool for helping remove past traumas and other obstacles to wellness. The healthy vibrant flow of energy through the physical body leads to greater vitality, joy and peace of mind for the Qigong practitioner. Spiral Qigong can be a spiritual as well as physical exercise promoting intuitive dreaming and fostering direct connection with Source. Spiral Qigong, the tarot shows, is an easy to learn practice that accelerates the evolution of consciousness towards fulfilling our human potential.

Part III is the personal account of my spiral dreaming over a 10 year period. In fact, dreaming led me to Qigong. Inner awareness later showed me that by bridging the energies of heaven and earth through the body, spirals of transcendental energy would rise from the earth and awaken the consciousness of the body. As I practiced Spiral Qigong the quality of my dreams improved and my dream recall was greatly enhanced. Qigong and dreams together, what I refer to as Qigong Dreaming, became a purifying agent and a catalyst for tremendous self discovery and initiation. Dreams, I was surprised to discover, reflected the hidden wisdom of the alchemical arts as well as tarot illustrations. Lao Tzu taught that the doorway to the golden secret of all life leads to knowledge of virtues (*de*). *De* represents moral character and the qualities of kindness, compassion and benevolence. The Chinese character for *de* depicts 14 couples who come together with one heart and mind.[6] My training on virtues came through my dreams. Their esoteric lessons are described alongside the remaining 14 tarot cards of the major arcana showing a progressive evolution or spiritualization of the soul. Serendipitously, these cards seemed to arrange themselves as if by divine order. They show inherent balance between the virtues of *yin* (the feminine side of spirituality) and the virtues of *yang* (the masculine side of spirituality).

When dreams are discussed in the presence of others, the dialogue is believed to benefit the community as well as the dreamer. Supporting this idea, I describe a total of 77 dreams (note that 7+7=14, the number of couples in the *de*), which I believe can offer interesting insight for anyone on the path to greater self understanding. These tarot dreams highlight the benefits of paying attention to, interpreting and following the guidance of dreams: greater health, joy and peace of mind. The symbolism I discuss may help dream workers delve deeper into their own dream analysis, offering greater understanding into the universal language of dreams. I have included this personal dialogue in the hope of validating the experience of others who unknowingly receive profound and benevolent dream messages. My lessons learned can help dispel fears about nightmares and concerns about sexually explicit content. Dreams that may appear confusing from a limited Western cultural perspective become better understood once the ancient symbolism of Chinese Medicine and inner alchemy is objectively translated.

The Rider Waite tarot deck is a great accompaniment to this book. This resource can be purchased at most bookstores or easily found online. A copy of the major arcana illustrations referenced in this book can also be found at the website www.taooftarot.com. I encourage you to explore and record your own tarot dreaming as the alchemy of Spiral Qigong transforms you. The best life coaching is available through the internal guidance system of your own dreams. May each of you be empowered to discover your own inner light and in so doing move all of us towards the evolution of consciousness: one mind, one heart.

Part I:

Lao Tzu's Golden Secret of All Life

Chapter 1

The Fool

The first and sometimes the last card of the tarot's major arcana cards is the Fool. Rather than being foolish, however, I would suggest that the youth depicted as both the alpha and the omega is like Jesus Christ, the archetype for the spiritual adept. A spiritual adept is anyone who has passed all challenges; who understands the mysteries of reality; and who experiences a state of enlightened oneness with God.

Circular dome ceiling in the Chora Church in Istanbul, Turkey shows Mother Mary with Jesus in the center surrounded by twelve archangels. The Byzantine mosaics describe Christ as the Land of the Living and his Mother as the Container of the Uncontainable.

Hindu philosophy uses the term *avatar* to describe the incarnation of a deity or spirit into physical form.[4] This term is also used to reference the incarnations of God or highly spiritual teachers such as Jesus, Abraham, Muhammad, Shiva, Quetzalcoatl and Buddha.[5] The inner traditions of Chinese Medicine teach that whatever our religious background, we can all experience spiritual wisdom. The universal teachings of the Chinese Taoist philosopher Lao Tzu corresponds directly to the meaning of the Fool card. We each innately have everything we need within us to live healthy, happy and prosperous lives; we are already perfect. Returning to a state of childlike innocence through a practice like Qigong Dreaming, we remember who we truly are. Gaining knowledge of our greater self, we comprehend the divine light within.

The alchemical arts and alternate Christian spiritual practices were heavily censored by the Roman Catholic Church in the Middle Ages, the time when the tarot spread widely throughout Europe. Out of fear of torture and death, the arcane wisdom was hidden in symbolic format and subtly incorporated in story telling, visual art and written prose. Information was secretly passed to those able to decipher the meaning of the symbols. The tarot images are, I believe, a non-verbal means to pass along the Asian secrets to youthful long life and spiritual immortality. Spreading from the East, this wisdom influenced the major religions of the West. Internal cultivation techniques to create the elixir of life, the elusive fountain of youth and Holy Grail for vitality, prosperity and everlasting life, are symbolically represented in the tarot through picture form. For as the Chinese proverb goes, 'One picture is worth 10,000 words'.

The 22 major arcana cards of the tarot are represented by a Roman numeral except for the Fool card. Directly above the image of the Fool there is a black circle or zero. The number zero has no Roman numeral equivalent. The Fool card is thus an anomaly as the remaining cards follow a set format. The black circle as zero is, therefore, a clue marking an important distinction.

Heavenly wheel upon the ceiling of the Sultan Ahmed Mosque, also known as the Blue Mosque in Istanbul, Turkey.

The Chinese character for the number zero means emptiness. Emptiness (*wu*) is 'the Way' back home to our innate nature. Clearing the mind of thoughts is the basis of spiritual practice.[6] This was the original purpose of Qigong practice.[7] Qigong movement exercise as a meditation helps individuals relax the intellect and be receptive to a higher power. Qigong is prayer in motion and a means of letting go of the ego's control and limited vantage point. For when we can quiet the mental chatter, we create a space to receive the omnipotent power of pure awareness. This eternal Presence, called the Tao in the East, is accessible through the consciousness of the body. Fostering inner development, regular Qigong practice activates high frequency life force energies within the physical body. Through the alchemical process the physical becomes enlightened and eventually spiritualized. Transmuting the physical body into a body of light we awaken to our full potential.

In spontaneous Qigong, we allow the radiance of the universe to channel through and move our bodies unconsciously. Typically stifled by cultural dictates growing up, we begin to return to the naturalness of the self. By allowing the body to move on its own accord, higher quality thoughts and images are generated and become accessible consciously to guide us. This Qigong Dreaming is how we access the wisdom of the Tao; we harmonize our bodies and hearts, cleansing away limiting beliefs, dualistic thinking, emotional constraints and physical toxins stored within the cell receptors of the body.[8] For when we conform to peer, family and societal pressures, we block the free flow of vital energy or '*qi*', thus blocking our intuitive gifts and potentially compromising our health and happiness. Using Qigong to release old subconscious programs and patterns, our cells themselves enliven and can dance to a higher vibration. Regaining our innate instincts, we embrace life and enjoy greater peace. As research in biomedicine is now showing, when we feel good, we strengthen our bodies and connect with God.[8]

In *The Records of the Historian,* Confucius speaks of his visit with Lao Tzu saying, 'Today I have seen Lao Tzu and I can say that I have seen the Dragon'. Dragons, a symbol of the Tao in Asia, are divine and angelic beings. Incorporated in Chinese art, they are found coiled among the clouds surrounding the flaming pearl of spiritual illumination. A dragon or serpent in circular form creates the Ouroborus, the ancient revolving symbol of cyclical change leading to primordial unity in many cultures. The Ouroborus dragon represents humanity's union with the cosmos in many forms: mandalas, megalithic arrangements of early civilizations, circular cathedral windows, Pueblo and Australian Aboriginal sand paintings, celestial zodiac wheels, Native American dream catchers and much more. In Taoism, the Ouroborus represents the unifying life force of central energy (*chong qi*) and the transcendental power of the Tao. Described as whirling emptiness, central *qi* is created when the energies of heaven and earth merge together. Applied to the human body, central *qi* is commonly known in tantric practices as the kundalini or coiled serpent. Working with central *qi,* through the body-minded practice which I term Spiral Qigong, the tarot teaches a method for spiritual awakening. The tarot shows that the O-uroborus is a powerful tool for connecting with the infinite intelligence of the universe and finding liberation from one's problems.

Dragons in China represent spiritual energy, the direction of the East and the time of dawn when the sun begins its ascent into the sky. Earthbound, dragons are the element of wood and the greenness of plants in the springtime when new growth sprouts upward towards the warmth of the sun to flourish once more. The dragon of the East is characterized by a rising upward movement of *yang* or masculine energy. As a member of the Hermetic Order or the Golden Dawn and teacher of alchemy, A.E. Waite, the originator of the cards, would have known of symbolic meanings. The dragon power as a symbol and means to spiritual wisdom is subtly included in the imagery of Waite's Fool card in a number of ways. First, the Fool is a young male representing *yang* energy. He lifts his countenance and chest upward towards the sky to emphasize the rise of spiritual energies. As a symbol of spring he wears images of vegetation such as leaves and fruit upon his clothes and hat. The youth represents the plant kingdom and the element most associated with the spiraling and transcendental central *qi* in Chinese Medicine.

> Chinese dragons are often depicted amongst spiraling clouds guarding the pearl of spiritual illumination in Asian art.

The youth in the Fool card appears to be opening his heart. In Chinese theory, the heart is the heavenly abode of Spirit and the spiritual center of our being. All the other organs and their respective officials take direction from this Emperor of the body.

Likewise, the purification of the heart leads to all healing as every disease is, in a sense, related to the heart.[7] Our youth in the card carries a single white rose. This object is the tool of spiritual cultivation and the symbol of transcendental energies in Qigong theory.[7] Insight into what this tool for spiritual development actually is can be found on the young man's other side. In his right hand the youth carries a wooden pole with a red sack upon the end. The red filled container at the top of the pole represents the ascension of central *qi* or kundalini energies from the womb like energy container of the lower abdomen (as well as the sacred blood of Christ within a holy drinking vessel). The physical has, therefore, become spiritualized through Qigong techniques. Transformed by the rise of whirling energies the individual pictured has through his practice created the golden immortal body. We see that he has discovered the secret of eternal life by the insertion of gold upon the apex of the pole. Unable to rust, tarnish, or decay, gold contains the divine nature of the sun. Found in alchemical illustrations and manuscripts, gold is the highest state of a metal and the goal of the transformative alchemical arts. It is a symbol of enlightenment and immortality achieved.[9]

Working with life force energy or qi during Qigong practice under the trees. People often meet in the parks in China to practice Qigong together.

The basis of health and wholeness from a traditional Asian philosophy comes from our innate correspondence with nature. Everything within us (the microcosm) is reflected in the world around us (the macrocosm). The universe and our bodies are synchronized from this holistic approach, with everything composed of five elements. The elements of wood (plants), fire, earth, metal (stone and mountains) and water found in our environment also make up the physical, psychological and spiritual aspects of ourselves. The ancient Chinese shamans compared the heart as spiritual center of the body to the spirit of the sun.[7] This explains the placement of the sun in the card's background and the fact that the red feather on the youth's head floats to this 'Central Sun'. What appears to be two and separate – youth and sun, physical and spiritual – are in reality unified as one.

The imagery of the Fool is reminiscent of the constellation of Orion the Hunter being followed faithfully by his dog Sirius known as Canis Major in the night sky. Similarly, the young man in Waite's image walks forward in serene confidence with his canine friend for company. Dogs are known to be carrion eaters and have universal symbolism as guides to the dead in the underworld. Buried in tombs of ancient China and South America, they were placed in burial chambers to lead the deceased to the heavens. Deified in India as an aspect of Shiva the Destroyer, they were liberators of the soul.[10] Similarly, in ancient Egypt, the jackal headed god, Anubis, is known as the Opener of 'the Way'. A descendent of an earlier dog deity from Central Asia, according to world renowned Egyptologist E. A. Wallis Budge, Anubis taught humanity how to transform the physical body and attain immortality. Priests wearing jackal headed masks prepared the mummified dead through extensive ritual for their journey to the stars.

In Greek mythology, it is the three-headed dog, Cerberus, whose tail is likened to the serpent, who guards the entrance to the Land of the Dead until the hero Hercules, as a final labor, brings him into the light of day.[11] In an 18th century interpretation by writer Zachary Grey, the three heads of Cerberus represent the past, present and future that devour everything. It is only through Herculean efforts that one can be 'victorious over Time' and find true liberation.[11] In the 20th century, Jung highlighted the importance of exploring the personal dreamscape to liberate the splintered aspects of the individual that have unknowingly been relegated to the underworld, the shadows of the subconscious. The journey to healing is, therefore, a journey to uncover that which is hidden within. Becoming fully conscious, we rediscover our wholeness as represented by the circle of the zero. Seen as white or uncolored, the dog in the Waite card is a symbol of pure light of the higher self. Without burden or karma, the dog represents spiritual perfection obtained in physical form.

Lao Tzu taught that integrating the intellect with the intuitive mind leads to a life filled with synchronicity and the Trinity where heaven, earth and humankind are united within.[6] Jung defined synchronicity as meaningful coincidence or the interrelationship between psyche and matter. Alchemists also knew that nothing occurs by happenstance and that everything has meaning.[3] The inherent interconnectedness of the universe comes at crucial phases to guide us towards individuation and the fulfillment of destiny.[12] This mystical dream like reality becomes more apparent when we practice Qigong. Life becomes a fluid and seamless state of existence where things come together serendipitously and fall into place with natural ease.

For example, the following quote by Edward Feller appeared fortuitously at the community center where I was working at the time of this chapter writing. It demonstrates the meaning of the Fool as spiritual adept. Refusing to conform to cultural or restrictive religious constraints, one may appear foolhardy. Knowing the esoteric secrets of life, however, one lives in a permanent state of joyful bliss with the Tao, untroubled by public perception. Spiritual faith built on personal experience builds trust in the divine will of God, whatever the outcome.

When you come to the end of
all the light you know,

and are about to step off into the
darkness of the unknown,
FAITH is knowing
one of two things will happen:
There will be something solid to stand on
or, you will be taught to fly

Chapter 2

The Magician

Often following the Fool in the deck is another male figure, that of the Magician. This character is associated with a god rather than a human being. Here is the ancient Greek Messenger of the gods, Hermes, whom Waite's organization entitled the Hermetic Order of the Golden Dawn centered on. Hermes – equivalent to the Egyptian jackal-headed deity Anubis[2] – was the white dog in the last card. In the Magician card he has taken central stage to highlight his importance. Hermes, or Mercury as he was known to the Romans, was guide to the subterranean Underworld and the hidden subconscious recesses of the mind. Known as the Father of Alchemy, Hermes Trisgemistrus or Thrice Great Hermes is the symbol of the death to rebirth process of transformation in the human body and within the earth (his stone markers on European roadways channeled high frequency energies to sacred sites). Hermes was the god within to the Gnostics[13] who taught how to change a person into a god. Through the alchemical process associated with Hermes, certain Christian sects believed they could become one or equal with Christ.[13]

The ancient Greek god of alchemy Hermes pictured here with wings of enlightenment atop his head in Istanbul, Turkey.

The Magician card carries the Roman numeral I. One in Chinese numerology is a symbol of unity. Confucius said we combine *yin* and *yang* to return to the Tao.[7] It is through unity that we activate the whirling emptiness of central *qi* and reunite with the transcendence of God. Defined simply, *yin* is the feminine qualities of dark, moist and cool and is likened to the shady side of the mountain, while *yang* is represented by the masculine qualities of light, dry and warm and is the sunny side of the mountain. Chinese theory teaches that we need a balance of *yang* and *yin,* masculine and feminine, conscious and unconscious, outward and inward, upward and downward for health, stability and harmonious existence.

Prior to the well known *Taiji yin yang* symbol, unity was represented in ancient Chinese artwork by the image of the spiral.[7] The spiral represents the transformational quality of the cycles of life. The moving inward or returning aspect of the cycle allows one to let go of perceived challenges or limitations on the journey to the center of the higher self. From this center comes the expressive movement of the spiral stretching itself outward. Having transcended the old, it can expand its trajectory wider than ever before. We may already be home and one with Spirit as described by the Fool card. Exemplified by the Magician card is the journey or the way to consciously knowing this truth.

The cycling Ouroborus' represents the movement of cosmic energy around the human body. The ascent of energy up the vertebral column of the spine is along the energy pathway in what the Chinese refer to as the *Du Mai* or Governing Vessel (GV). This major energy meridian depicts the phase of ascension and is the 'Root of all *Yang*' in the body. The opposing downward flow of energy along the front centerline of the body travels along

> A triple spiral marks the entrance stone at Newgrange, Ireland. On the winter solstice the rising sun (yang) illuminates the otherwise darkened chamber within (yin) in what may have been a spiritual rebirth ritual. Threshold spiral markings are also found at sacred sites in Europe, Mexico, China and Egypt.

the energy pathway termed the *Ren Mai* or Conception Vessel (CV). It represents the phase of manifestation or creative potential of the cycle. The CV is the 'Root of all *Yin*' in the body. Together the GV and CV unite to form an integral circular unit of flow called the microcosmic orbit. Building and refining the healthy flow of energy that mirrors the cosmic flow of the universe, we create a circular doorway – the Ouroborus – a reflection of the Universal Tao leading us back to health and wellness.

Lao Tzu taught that through inner awareness (*you*), we gain access to the dream state. Symbolized by the number one, thoughts and images arise as the appearance of initial intelligence.[6] Getting back into our body system is a means to promote dreaming and intuition. Mindful as the body moves spontaneously, we are receptive to divine insight and lucid dream revelation in Spiral Qigong. We become through our practice messengers of divine will, like the god Hermes.

Lao Tzu stated in *The Dao De Jing* that the state between zero (emptiness) and one (inner awareness) is the doorway to the golden secret of all life (*xuan*). The primary energy channel of the human body is called the Central Channel (*Chong Mai*). It is the most important energy channel of the body and the focus of Qigong cultivation techniques.[14] Located between the GV and CV, it is what I believe to be the source of the golden secret of all life. The Central Channel is a vehicle for uniting heaven and earth in order to activate the central *qi's* transcendent force within humanity and physical matter. It is also the energetic pathway connecting the three internal treasures or *dan tian* of the body. Thrice-great, like Hermes, this Trinity is found in the centers of the lower abdomen, chest and head. Harmonized and aligned through Qigong, the three *dan tian* create an 'elixir field'. This clue remains from ancient times, that the cycle of life-death-rebirth can be transcended and eternal life achieved through regular internal cultivation practice. The Central Channel is the vertical alignment with infinite Spirit, as symbolized by the crystal wand and the number 1 of the Magician card.

Depicted in the Magician card is the Ouroborus biting its tail and draped around the Magician's waist. In Chinese Medicine, the Belt Channel (*Dai Mai*) encircles the waist like a belt. This energy channel modulates the vertical flow of life force energy in the remaining energy pathways of the body. Thought by some to hold the karma of one's ancestral past,[15] the central *qi*'s counterclockwise movement can unlock and transmute energy obstacles and limitations held within the energy of the body. The serpent spiral applied to the body is the basis of the inner alchemical works. Purification techniques will facilitate ascension and unity consciousness as demonstrated by the infinity symbol above the Magician's head. The human body, the spiraling serpent and the infinity symbol put together create the wand of Hermes called the *caduceus*. The *caduceus* is the international symbol of health, wholeness and wisdom in the medical profession as well as Hermes' alchemical tool for turning physical objects

Author dreams of pulling a rock encircled by a snake out of the ground on winter solstice near Lake Titicaca in Peru. Dreams of working with and fixing energy ley lines of the earth at sacred sites around the world soon followed.

Jesus like the Magician is often pictured with red and white roses, colors associated with the alchemical arts.

into gold.

In the Waite Magician card, the right hand is held up high and is holding what looks like a double terminated crystal, while the left hand is held close to earth and pointing downward with the index finger. Crystals and the color white reflect the element of metal in Chinese theory and represent the direction of the West. Metal is the time of late afternoon when the sun sets and descends below the horizon. It is also the season of autumn when the leaves fall from the trees to earth. The downward descent of West energies is represented by the celestial tiger in Qigong theory. Depicted with white with black stripes, *yin* and *yang*, earth and heaven are in balance. The tiger represents the descent of divine knowledge into physical form. It is the *yin* or feminine aspect of the great cycle of energy. In matriarchal societies, it is the Divine Goddess. In Christianity, it is known as the Holy Spirit.[13]

The caduceus showing two snakes spiraling up a central rod was a symbol of Hermes the Greek messenger god. Some date the origins of the potential Mesopotamian symbol to 3000-5000 BCE. Applied to the body it shows the rise of central qi kundalini energies along the Central Channel.

The *yin* quality of the Magician card is reinforced by the downward-pointed index finger. By this gesture, the Magician directs the energies of the large intestine, which flows through this finger, downward. The large intestine is a metal organ whose function is to release the impure from the body. This is the benevolent predatory nature also associated with the celestial tiger. The importance of cleansing the body through death and rebirth is the alchemical process for biological, psychological and spiritual growth. This is shown in the Magician card with the use of white lilies. This flower is associated with death and funerals. However, lilies are only found upon the ground in this card. Death is only a construct of our earthly reality. Intentionally missing amongst the flowers above, the eternal aspect of the soul and our spiritual reality is also highlighted.

Autumn is also the time of harvest when we receive from the spiraling cornucopia of nature's bounty. The downward *yin*, thus, also represents the manifestation or the stepping down of Source (nonbeing) into physical form (being) leading to all of creation or what Lao Tzu referred to as 'the ten thousand things'. Manifestation is a creative and fertile process as seen by the flowering red roses. Growing both above and below, the blooming roses demonstrate the link established by the Magician between the transcendent reality above and the immanent reality below. In so doing, the omnipotence of the eternal Tao can be channeled down to earthly reality to transform the mundane.

> The cornucopia or horn of plenty associated with the Greek goddess Fortuna is a reminder of the abundance and fertility associated with the spiral symbol.

The Magician is someone aware of the mystical workings of magic. We are all involved in creating our physical experience; however, creating life experiences without awareness is most common. Science is finding that we attract to ourselves those situations and people that reflect what we believe, think and feel.[8] 'Where the mind goes, the *qi* follows' is how we express this concept in Qigong. A low density internal state will attract lower vibrational experiences of struggle, dis-ease and distress. Higher vibrational beliefs, thoughts and emotions attract harmony, health and bliss into our lives. It is not a matter of luck. If we want to attract constructively, we need to clear the negative subconscious programming held within the physical body and judgments from the conscious mind. Knowing this, we can choose to take greater responsibility for our lives. Working with central *qi*, we can transform our baser metals (destructive tendencies) and turn them into alchemical gold (higher self). Little by little, we can clear out the accumulated garbage that bogs down the energy flow of the body and wake up to our conscious involvement in creation. Manifesting conscientiously, we avoid creating for the sake of the ego. The ego will be overly attached to a desired result and will not understand the big picture of what is best for the situation. Personal will in conflict with divine will leads to dissatisfaction and creates negative karma. Working in harmony with the Tao, on the other hand, is the making of miracles. Being empty of attachments and fears, we remain neutral like the direction and facial expression of the Magician in this card. Channeling down the Holy Spirit through our hearts, we focus this energy towards the situation at hand. Aligning our God-self, we know that whatever the outcome, it is of the highest wisdom and benefit. Miracles are about letting go and letting God's pure consciousness flow.

> In the Karnak temple complex in Egypt walking counterclockwise around the scarab statue is believed to increase fertility and manifest one's dreams. Able Muslims pilgrimage to Saudi Arabia to walk several counter clockwise turns around the Kaaba stone.

The divine speaks and communicates chiefly through the world of dreams in what the Catholic Church calls *somnia a Deo missa*.[3] Lao Tzu likewise asserts that virtues come from listening to dreams and following the Tao.[6] Similar to the Tao, the Australian Aborigines say the sacred Dreamtime, or *Tjukurpa,* is the ever present and eternal way of life. Represented by the Cosmic Rainbow Serpent, the Dreamtime teaches about right living and interrelationships.[16] By uniting conscious (*yang*) and subconscious (*yin*) aspects of mind and body, we connect the left and right hemispheres of the brain and channel in what Jung described as the universal and symbolic language of the collective unconscious. Synonymous with nature, according to Jung, dreaming is intrinsic with Qigong. It is one way we can experience awareness of the Absolute.

Spiral Qigong facilitates lucid dreaming and conscious dream recall. Working consciously with the Dreamtime, Spiral Qigong provides the opportunity to resolve negative issues and memories held in the mind and body. We can work through our nightmares, resolving issues in the state of nonbeing before they have a chance to manifest as learning opportunities in our physical lives. Lucid dream work is a gentle and easy means to complete our karmic homework and resolve our issues. It is an amazing form of untapped potential and healing in our lives.

The primordial couple is common to many creation myths and wisdom teachings around the world. In Genesis of the Old Testament Adam *yang* and Eve *yin* are originally united within the Garden of Eden. They together experience unity with the undifferentiated oneness of God in a paradise reality. Eve ate an apple from the Tree of Knowledge. Like the *fall*ing leaves of autumn, the serpentine life force energy descends from heaven down the tree and slithers upon the earth. This descent from the spiritual to the physical led to humankind's ability to give birth and be a creative force in the world. No wonder the biblical name for Eve means Mother of All Living.[13] However, the ability to

> Fuxi and Nuwa are the primordial couple of ancient China often pictured with intertwining dragon or fish tails. Similar to the description of central qi they spiral upwards uniting the earth (white) below with the Central Sun (red). Holding the carpenter's square and compass the two figures bring harmony to the universe. The square and compass remain important symbols to modern day Freemasons who recognize the mythical dimension of reality and continue the Great Architect of the Universe's work.

create and live in the temporal world is painful when individuals become cut off from intuitive knowledge of their original spiritual reality. Living in the physical world without the personal experience of divine insight leads to the illusion of separation from Source. Rational thinking supersedes intuitive faculties in a material focused world. Hence, Adam and Eve, now representing opposing dualistic forces forget their original connection to God and are self exiled. They project their perceived separation onto their outer world of experience. The couple believes they have left the garden of abundance and see only desert and hardship around them. They have forgotten how to return to the Tree of Life in the center of the garden. Not knowing that the Tree of Life is symbolic of the energetic connection with Source within themselves they miss the opportunity to reunite with their innate oneness and transcend their dis-ease. They seem stuck in the fear based illusion of good vs. evil. However, there is hope for humanity as a future descendent, Jesus of Nazareth, symbolically connects with the transcendental reality when he ascends the wooden cross (comparable to the rise of central *qi* within the Central Channel) and becomes the Christ-ed. His resurrection gives the promise of eternal life to others.

Spiral Qigong, in brief, is a tool to help people embrace their bodies and live healthy, fulfilling lives. Unlocking intuition and dreaming, it is a means to heal and unify mind, body and spirit, and, for the spiritual minded, to return to oneness consciousness with the Infinite. The symbolic objects on the table of the Magician card reflect the process of awakening through inner cultivation.

The inner awareness of the Tao experienced through dreaming and intuition is represented by the metal element, the sword in this card. The process: Clear emotional blocks from the subconscious and the cells of the body liberating the instinctual aspect of the *yin* soul (*po*), the corporeal or body soul.

The wooden staff on the table depicts emptiness and spiritual nature through right action (wood element). The process: Clear the attachments of ego, judgments and karma from mental thinking to strengthen the *yang* soul (*hun*), the evolutionary soul in Chinese tradition.

The golden chalice in the sacrament of the Eucharist represents union with God through symbolic consumption of the blood and body of Christ.[9] Authors of Holy Grail legends of 14th century Europe spread the secrets of achieving the perfected human body through kundalini and alchemical activation.[17] This wisdom was passed by the Sufis, who learned internal cultivation techniques from China, India and Egypt.[18] The golden vessel on the Magician's table represents the receptive Central Channel of the enlightened human or the golden immortal body. Blending fire and water together, we can transcend to higher levels of consciousness through dreaming and reunite with the eternal. The process: Clear the Central Channel through Qigong practice to unite the soul with Spirit.

The five elements described in the Chinese Medical Classics, *Nei Jing* and *Nan Jing,* illustrate the balanced cyclical movement of the elements through the pentacle shape.[19] The star image upon the golden coin of the Magician card also depicts the balance of the five elements. The five circular movements of the Tao create the elements of water, fire, wood, metal and earth. The fifth and final stage of the Tao reflects the element of earth and the color yellow or gold. Earth is the central position of stillness within the central *qi's* whirling movement.[12] When the four elements or directions are in harmony, they form what the alchemists refer to as the gold growing deep within the center of the earth. Unlocking spiritual energy within matter is partaking of what is described in ancient prophesies as return of the Golden Age. The process: Be an open channel conducting heavenly energies to earth. Awakening the energy lines of the planet facilitating harmony and peace for all.

PART II:

Sacred Serpent Spiral Qigong

Chapter 3

The Hermit

Mircea Eliade writes, in *A History of Religious Ideas,* that the Chinese ideogram for an Immortal (*xian*) suggests a Hermit. The Hermit card represents the spiritual qualities of inner cultivation techniques leading to transcendence. Vitality and long life can be obtained through Qigong. The ultimate aim of practice, however, is to return to the Heavenly Realm of the Immortals high upon the mountain peaks and amongst the clouds. The immortal Hermit of this card has achieved eternal life characterizing one who lives in harmony with the totality of the Tao. Maintaining awareness of the innate oneness behind creation, living Immortals spend time meditating to be a benevolent influence upon humanity.[9]

The Hermit in this card represents the qualities of the mind used for relaxation and visualization in Qigong. Imitating the movements of animals and imagining oneself in and part of different natural settings such as the ocean or a forest floor we connect with different aspects of our own inner nature. Self discovery is achieved through communion with that which we might label as other in the natural world since everything in our external reality is also found within. The power of intention is also utilized to direct energy to key acupoints and body parts to help clear and strengthen the energy of the body during meditative movements. Even without physical movement, however, Qigong is said to be about 70 per cent effective as a visualization.[21] This demonstrates the strong influence of the mind in healing.

The energy of mental consciousness, known as *shen,* is the subtle *yang* energy of the heavens. *Shen* Spirit is one of the three internal treasures of the human body and corresponds to the energies of the Central Sun. This spiritual energy is stored in the center of the brain within an energy field called the upper *dan tian*.

In Chinese art, celestial energies are represented by the color blue. The robes of the Hermit in this card reflect the blue color of the sky showing divine influence. The Hermit holds a lantern directing the light of consciousness downward through his intention. He has drawn in his spiritual light by closing his eyes and is gently guiding the energy through the head and down the Central Channel depicted here as the wooden pole. It is at the crown of his head, particularly acupoint GV-20 or Hundred Meeting Point (*Bai Hui*), that the Hermit expands his conscious connection to Source energy and becomes a channel for Spirit. GV-20 is the upper axis of the Central Channel in the body.[19] Similarly, the Hermit's pointed hat, like those worn by wizards, witches and school dunces of the past, was believed to help spiral in the intelligence of the Universe.[2]

Guiding the *qi* or life force energy downwards through the upper *dan tian* in the head, the Qigong practitioner activates this spiritual center facilitating transpersonal awareness, divine insight and sacred dreaming. Qigong practitioners sometimes also guide life force energies into a point on the forehead called the Heavenly Collector (*Tian Mu*). This point is an external link to the upper *dan tian*. Its position is shown in this card where the Hermit's forehead contacts the pole. From this location, *qi* is directed down the Central Channel and into the lower *dan tian* of the abdomen.

Description of how to do Spiral Qigong

Before beginning Spiral Qigong, determine the type of music you would most enjoy moving to at this time. The choice may vary and change depending on your mood and what you feel like in the moment. It can be anything that makes you feel good, sensuous, strong, creative, playful, spiritually inspired, relaxed, or emotionally fluid. Check in and access what your soul is yearning for. If you feel a preference to practice Qigong in silence, that is perfectly fine as well. Let your intuitive mind and heart guide your decision.

Go to the place you would like to practice and get into a comfortable position. Bring the tip of your tongue upwards to gently connect with the upper palate just behind the upper teeth. This connects the GV and CV Channels initiating the flow of energy along the microcosmic orbit. Bring a smile upward from your heart to your eyes and out to the universe. Relax the focus of your gaze, slowly closing your eyes and bringing in your spiritual light. Relax the body part by part. Working downward from the top of the head, let go of any tensions and tightness held there by gently bringing the mind's attention to each successive area. Spend a few moments connecting with the energy of the head, neck, shoulders, upper arms, elbows, forearms, wrists, hands, fingers, chest, waist, lower abdomen, upper back, middle back, lower back, pelvic girdle, thighs, knees, legs, ankles, feet and toes.

Bring a little extra attention to some of the joints of the body. The joints (*guanjie*) act as spiritual gates, allowing body parts to move with the universal rhythm of *qi*.[7] Prime and loosen the joints by letting them begin to move and express themselves. Focus on allowing the head, shoulders, elbows and wrists, the hips, ankles and the whole spine to let go and play for a few minutes.

Now, visualize yourself in a beautiful place in nature filled with wondrous *qi*. Any special place to you, real or imaginary, that helps you feel and experience a light and youthful heart is ideal. Spontaneously allow the scenery details to present themselves and change, knowing they are being directed by your higher self. You may be in the mountains, near the ocean, at a forest meadow, with or without wildlife nearby. Increase your awareness and connection to the location using your inner senses for added details. Be aware of any sounds or smells of this special place. Use your tactile senses to feel the earth between your toes, the wind on your skin, the sun or moonlight shining down upon you. Note how it feels to move and explore your environment through the mind's sense of touch.

When you are ready to begin, bring your mind's attention to the center of your palms, the acupoint known as *Lao Gong*. Turn your palms forward and imagine yourself holding a ball of vibrant energy or *qi* in front of your body. Holding this ball of swirling energy, you may have a sense of its pure vibration and harmonious perfection as you tune into and sense it. While focusing on the palms of your hands and with relaxed arms and hands, use your shoulders to slowly lift the ball of *qi* upward towards the heavens allowing it to absorb the energies of the stars, the moon, the sun and the celestial bodies of the heavens. When your hands reach the level of your ears, relax your wrists turning your palms downward. Bending your elbows to the sides, slowly and naturally guide the ball of *qi* down through GV 20 at the top of the head and into the central pillar of the Central Channel. Moving your hands softly downward in front of the body, feel or imagine the energy going through the middle of the head, through the center of the chest and into the lower *dan tian* at the center of the lower abdomen.

Chapter 4

The Star

The upper body is *yang* or masculine while the lower body is *yin* or feminine, according to Chinese theory. Having moved the energy down through the top of the head and to the lower abdomen in Qigong practice, we have moved from *yang* to *yin*. Leaving the elderly wise male figure of the Hermit we move to address the Star card, which depicts a young maiden bending close to earth. As the heavenly energies continue to pour into the Central Channel, they are guided down to the most important storage location for our physical vitality, the lower *dan tian*.

The lower *dan tian* is located about two inches below the navel and within the pelvic cavity of the lower abdomen. Acting like a container or vase, it is a reservoir for storing the sexual feminine essence of the body. Directing energies to the lower *dan tian* is a critical component of Qigong practice. Within this gravitational center of the body, the *jing* is stored and refined for physical vitality, youthful appearance, creative potency and spiritual growth.

Legs partially separated, the maiden in the Star card opens up the important acupoint CV-1, called Meeting of Yin (*Hui Yin*), found between the legs at the perineum. Its precise location is between the anus and sexual organs. A very important acupoint in Taoist meditation, it is the lower position on the Central Channel or axis of the body.[19] It is also the *yin* extremity of the microcosmic orbit linking and strengthening the energy flow between the CV and GV in addition to the energy flow of the Central Channel. (The *yang* extremity occurs at the tongue placement on the upper palate just behind the teeth.) As the first point on the Conception Vessel or CV-1, it is the only point that through stimulation strengthens all three important energetic pathways. This is another correspondence in Chinese Medicine to the Holy Trinity within.

An alternate name for CV-1 is Metal Gate. This is the location likened to the entrance of the Queen Mother's kingdom.[12] The Queen Mother (*Xiwangmu*), also known as the Queen of the West, is the primary Taoist goddess and represents the element of metal and the quality of introspection. This mythical Chinese figure later associated with Kwan Yin descends from her mountain top to guide and assist virtuous individuals. Offering a white hollow tube (as a metaphor for the Central Channel), she bequests gifts of power, intuitive wisdom and immortality.[22] The Queen Mother is a symbol of the *yin* and feminine spiritual force of the Tao. She is synonymous with the archetype of the Great Goddess of many spiritual traditions and the Holy Spirit. We cannot intellectually comprehend the *yang* aspect of the Eternal. Lao Tzu states in the *Dao De Jing* that he does 'not know its name' but refers to it as 'formless and perfect'.[20] However, awareness of *yin* Spirit is experienced through dreaming and mystical insights. Activating CV-1 through Qigong, we open a doorway of awareness to the hidden reality of existence. The word *dan* from *dan tian* also means cinnabar – a red metallic substance used in alchemy to produce mercury.[20] Mercury, equal to gold in symbolic power, represents the eternal and immutable oneness of the Tao.[20] The Central Channel is the place where all three *dan tian* (physical, emotional and mental) are unified. It is the inner alchemical mixing ground of the Taoist Sages. This is the energetic seat for spiritual regeneration and kundalini awakening. Activating the sacred serpent spiral within the Central Channel is a means of tremendous healing and spiritual transformation.

The Chinese character for blood depicts a vase filled with blood.[12] In ancient times, ceremonial vessels of blood were used ritually to summon and nourish the spirits.[12] Through the external application of blood, objects became energetically animated and enlivened.[23] The water poured from the red vases in the Star card is comparable to the outpouring of ceremonial blood, particularly menstrual blood coming from the womb. Menstrual blood originally had sacred and magical powers among many traditional earth-centered cultures, including the Chinese. The Dakotan word *Waken,* meaning 'spiritual, consecrated, wonderful, incomprehensible', is also a term that describes women who are menstruating.[23] The Polynesian term for menstrual blood was originally associated with reverence and awe.[23]

Red vase sculpture from the Bronze Age of present day Turkey shows the creative potential as the outpouring of a red spiral stream from the Goddess.

The increased blood flow to the lower abdomen during menstruation would naturally increase the energy field of the lower *dan tian,* helping awaken the cinnabar field of the Central Channel. Our ancestors were likely more aware of this intuitively than we are today. The descending flow of what was known as regenerative blood would symbolize the downward flow of blessings from heaven. The woman in the Star card is pouring her waters onto the land as a symbol of fertility. She is also adding to the large water body and generating circular ripples upon its surface. This outward spiraling effect represents the body's interface with the collective unconscious and the interchange of energy between the Tao and the physical world.

The *Chong Mai* is known as the Central Channel in Chinese medicine, but the word *Mai* has additional meanings. *Mai,* meaning blood vessel, is composed of two characters; the one on the left depicts the ideogram for body tissue, muscle, or flesh; the character on the right describes the currents of water flowing deep within the earth.[24] From this description it can be surmised that within our blood vessels flow subtle currents of energy equaling and interacting with those within the earth: ley lines in the West and dragon lines in the East. According to dowsers and *feng shui* practitioners, the movement of underground rivers generates magnetic currents.[25] Potent sites of harmonious *yin* and *yang* balance are found upon these dragon lines like acupuncture points on the energy channels of the body. The movement of central *qi* at these locations makes them sacred. Temples, megalithic structures and pyramids of China and other countries were intentionally built upon these holy positions to help increase productivity of the lands, enhance spiritual communion and benefit the local populations with their positive influence. Their vertical alignment helps channel and ground heavenly energies down to earth like the Central Channel of Qigong practitioners and steel needles used during acupuncture. When *yin* and *yang* unite and the five elements are in balance within, the Chinese alchemist brings order to the universe through his or her work. As ancient

Dream sketch of a bird drinking from a pool of water and creating ripples upon the surface. In dreams we likewise connect with the spiritual world and are nourished by the collective unconscious.

Aerial view of Nasca lines show a monkey with a spiral tail and large images of concentric circles. There are also spiral aqueducts remaining from the Nasca culture (300 BCE) in present day Peru.

Chinese alchemical art shows, the resulting elixir of life cascades down like flowing water below the alchemist's feet and into the earth.[9] The free flow of central *qi* within the Central Channel of a Qigong practitioner helps harmonize the dragon lines of the earth. As an authority on Chinese alchemist art explained, the elixir brings harmony and immortality onto everything it flows upon.[9]

The *Mai* is both the rhythmic pulsation from the heart contraction as well as the overall circulatory system of the blood.[26] The blood is believed to be the physical substance that helps anchor *shen* Spirit within the body. Its physical structure allows it to hold and distribute the electromagnetic impulse generated by the heart contraction. The electromagnetic fields generated by the movement of blood are similar to the geologic magnetic fluctuations created by water flowing within the earth. The Taoist sages knew this and taught that the blood received the royal seal of heaven when it became energetically spiritualized, passing through the heart. It was from the heart that the blood was believed to gain its redness, symbolizing transference of Spirit and spiritual fire-like attributes.[26]

The water flowing downward from the vase to the earth in the Star card brings to mind the rain as a fertility symbol in agricultural societies. *Ling,* as transmuted and spiritualized *jing* essence, represents the *yin* Spirit of the heart. It is the creative spiritual potency of the universe.[12] The Chinese character for *ling* depicts two female shamans dancing (perhaps as spontaneous movement) and summoning, through three mouths, the rain

> Sketches of Chinese alchemists often use Qigong hand positions of one palm facing up and the other down to form a human bridge between heaven and earth. Sometimes a stream flows beneath the alchemists' feet bringing order and harmony to the surrounding land.

Jesus with the same hand position as an Asian alchemist unites heaven and earth in this fresco of Judgment Day at the Chora Church in Turkey. A blood red stream flows between Jesus and His Mother then cascades into the earth to help others find spiritual freedom.

from heaven.[27] In ancient China it was the wise shaman whom people trusted to communicate knowledge from heaven. The mouth channels the voice of Spirit in Qigong.[7] A 4th century BCE text, *Conversations of the States,* explains that the mouth 'is the gate of the Three and the Five'; the five elements govern the workings of the universe and create the three layers of the universe.[7] The three layers of the universe are the Trinity: heaven, humanity and earth. They are reflected as the *shen, qi and jing* of the three *dan tian* within the body. When we align the three inner treasures within the Central Channel, we connect our heart Spirit through voice with the Cosmos.[7] And like the ancient shamans we become a channel for healing ourselves, others and the earth. The ancient shamans were able to call forth the blessings of heaven, as they were the original alchemists knowing the way to order and abundance on Earth[7].

Joseph Campbell explained that there are two ways of thinking about the Buddha: Buddha found his Buddha nature through meditation and he is the incarnation of Buddha consciousness and without meditating just knew it.[28] At birth, the baby Buddha is received by the gods on a golden cloth. He immediately stands up and takes seven steps. Similar to the Magician, he raises his right hand to heaven and lowers his left hand to the Earth. He then roars like a lion declaring 'Worlds above, worlds below, there's no one in the world like me!'[28] Buddha consciousness is equivalent to the living Christ consciousness found within everyone. It is about knowing you are 'it' and returning to the state of innocence of a newborn child.[28] The Buddha, known as Gautama, came as an adult to the tree in the center of the universe (Central Channel), called the immovable spot. Sitting in meditation, he is challenged by desire (*kama*), fear (*mara*) and finally social duty (*dharma*).[28] Confronted by the final challenge, the Buddha touches the earth with his hand, calling on the goddess Mother Universe, who in a voice of thunder proclaims his right to be there. At this point *dharma* departs respectfully and Guatama, fully enlightened, becomes Buddha, 'the Awakened one'.[20] Working with the transcendental central *qi* released from within the earth the Buddha purifies himself of his final challenge (choosing authenticity over doing things because one should) and returns to a state of wholeness.

Several days later a storm moves in and the serpent king, Mucalinda, rises from within the earth behind the Buddha's body, symbolically representing the flow of energy rising along the

> Statues of the Buddha often emphasizes the abundance of life force energy in the belly or lower dan tian. Statues of the Buddha are honored as reflections of our innate human potential for enlightenment.

Governing Vessel of the spine. Placing his hooded head over the Buddha, the serpent king protects him while the rains fall downward in front of the Buddha, along the Conception Vessel, until the storm is over. The serpent and rainfall at Buddha's illumination are synonymous with the flow of the microcosmic orbit of the body. Focusing inner cultivation within the Central Channel naturally frees up the circular flow of energy between the eternal and the physical.

Campbell described what he referred to as the two Buddhisms: the movement away from the field of time, or transcendent aspect of Buddhism, and the movement in the field of time, or the immanent manifestation aspect of Buddhism.[28] Enlightenment is living in the physical world without being moved. Having an awareness of the transcendental center of the Ouroborus while simultaneously experiencing nature's life cycles, we have what Buddhism refers to as 'joyful participation in the sorrows of the world.[28] Fundamentally, Buddhism, Taoism, Hinduism, the Mysteries of Greece and Egypt, the earth-centered cultures of Australia, Africa, North and South America and Jewish, Christian and Muslim traditions all reflect this universal truth. As the Japanese say, though there are many different paths to take, when you get to the top of the mountain, you see the same stars.

The Buddha took seven steps at birth and sat enlightened seven days when the serpent king arrived. There are seven stars in the Star card of Waite's deck as well. Seven in Chinese numerology is analogous to the seven stars of the Big Dipper. The spoon of the dipper contains the cosmic energy of the universe according to Chinese shamanic tradition and is the heart of heaven.[7] Ancient astronomers observed that the handle of the Big Dipper (three stars corresponding to the *dan tian* in Taoist thought) rotated in the night sky around a central fixed position, the North or Polestar. The Polestar is the upper central axis of the universe as GV-20 is the upper pole of the body. Taoist philosophers believe that the Big Dipper pours the celestial energies of the sky into the Central Channel via this acupoint at the top of the head.

The Big Dipper is also the source of individuality in Taoist theory. Having marked our essence at conception, we carry the imprint or royal seal of heaven upon our *jing* essence throughout our lifetime.[12] Defining our innate characteristics, it guides our destiny through lifetime events and intuitive promptings. The celestial rays of the heavens shine down our Central Channel like a flashlight illuminating our essence in the lower abdomen or lower *dan tian* of the body.[12] We enhance access to this light by clearing and strengthening the Central Channel through regular Qigong practice. Awakening and purifying intuition and dreaming, heaven can better guide us to our state of original authenticity before birth. We can return to a time when we were like the youthful maiden of this card, radiant like a star and unencumbered by external coverings.

In the background of the card, we see the image of a red bird atop a tree. This is the immortal mythological Phoenix, one of the four celestial animals of the sky. The Phoenix is the heart of the individual just as the Big Dipper is the heart of the universe in this microcosm to macrocosm correspondence.[7] The Phoenix represents the fire element in Chinese thought and is associated with the color red. While the Emperor is the dragon, the Empress is the phoenix in ancient times. As the main character in a ballet of the same name by Igor Stravinsky and based on a Russian folktale, the Firebird is the enchanted half woman - half bird who roams wild and free in the forest helping the hero and heroine (the pair of *yang* and *yin*) overcome danger and reunite, returning to oneness. Similarly, when the *yin* aspect of Spirit, called *ling,* helps awaken magical potency and personal guidance through dreaming, the *yin* and *yang* aspect of the soul are purified and reunited in the heart with Spirit. We can then experience joyful bliss and recognize that we are interfused with Tao.

In the *I Ching*, the number seven represents rebirth or recreation.[7] After a long and extended lifespan (varying in Egyptian, Greek and Chinese myth) the Phoenix dies in a flame of fire and regenerates anew from the ashes. This death to rebirth process reaffirms the alchemical transcendental meaning of this card; CV-1 as the Metal Gate is death as a gateway to rebirth.[7] The spiritual energy of the *yin* soul (*po*) is the body soul. Governing instincts and intuition, its Chinese character is translated as *white ghost*.[7] Ordinarily, the *yin* soul returns to the earth at death. However, when individuals who have cultivated their energies and purged and united their soul die, the soul ascends to heaven in a complete spiritual rebirth.[7]

There are seven aspects to the *yin* soul, according to Chinese theory, that relate to the seven emotions; fear, sadness, grief, anger, over thinking, shock and overexcitement are the seven internal causes of disease.[19] Prolonged, intense, unexpressed and unacknowledged emotions create imbalance, offsetting the life force energy of an individual. From an alchemical perspective, the emotions need to be purified for the physical body to be liberated. Seven appears to be a universally sacred number for the path to liberation in many traditions; there are seven chakras associated with the goddess Shakti in Tantric Hinduism, seven Stoles of the Egyptian goddess Isis, seven rays or sons of the goddess Sophia in Gnosticism, seven joys and sorrows of Mother Mary, seven colors to the Greek rainbow goddess Iris, seven departed demons of Mary Magdalene and seven dwarfs with Snow White. Seven days following the Buddha's birth, his mother Maya dies to be reborn as a god.[20] Joshua in the Bible also walks or spirals around the city of Jericho seven times before the walls (symbol of self constructed obstacles), made of *yin* metal, fall down.[29]

Awakening the sacred serpent spiral, we remove limiting beliefs, negative thoughts, addictions and suppressed emotions from the subconscious body. Like Jesus of Nazareth in Eph. 4:9, we must first descend into hell, to confront and transform our own inner issues, before we can ascend the seven steps to heaven, becoming Christed ourselves.[30]

In the Star card, there is a central bright golden star above the head of the maiden. In Greek mythology, the beautiful maiden Psyche, whose name translates as *soul*, overcomes numerous challenges put upon her by the Goddess of Love, Aphrodite. Through initiation, Psyche develops strength, maturity and individuation. Returning from the underworld, she completes her final task and is reunited with her husband Eros, the God of Love (from whom she had been forcibly separated from when she lost faith in him). Psyche is redeemed by her actions and made immortal by the king of the gods, Zeus. The reunion with her heavenly husband signifies the harmonizing of feminine and masculine traits within. From their alchemical sacred marriage or *hieros gamos*, the husband (*yang*) and wife (*yin*) produce a child, whose name is Joy. The golden star in this card represents a state of joy in the heart and the purity of soul achieved. We return to

In Greek mythology Psyche completing her initiatory tasks acquires her wings and becomes immortal like the gods. Does this story reflect our human potential?

joy and authentic living when we act spontaneously; we rebirth through the final stage of alchemy where soul and Spirit become one.

Description of how to do Spiral Qigong

Continue to guide the *qi* downward from the lower abdomen, down through CV-1 between the legs. Arms extend downwards and straighten as you continue to direct the *qi* with your mind's eye into the ground, between your feet and downward through the layers of the earth. Feel or imagine the energy entering the center or heart of the earth and gently rest your attention there.

Chapter 5

Temperance

In Taoist philosophy, it is the role of humankind to mediate between heaven and earth. Balancing the energies of heavenly *yang* and earthly *yin,* we find depicted in the Temperance card a neutral or androgynous angel or enlightened being. The whiteness of metal on the angel's clothing reflects a purified state. The triangle over the chest shows that the Trinity or three treasures are aligned and unified within the middle *dan tian.* The red wings of the Star card's Phoenix bird have now become integrated within. No longer is *yin* Spirit represented in the background as a bird high up in the tree. Instead, subject and object, self and other, matter and Spirit are together as one. In the Temperance card, the individual has rediscovered the divinity within and the interconnectedness of life. The solar *bindu* symbol on the forehead is another sign that the individual is consciously aware of this state of grace.

This statue of unknown origins depicts the spiral movement of the third eye, the chakra associated with inner sight and intuitive dreaming.

How did the individual achieve illumination? The answer to this question is found in the illustration on the card. The unusual placement of the angel's feet clues us into their mystical importance from a Taoist perspective. One foot is submerged in water while the other rests upon a rock near the bank; an odd posture to be sure. Our angel, however, is standing between the North or water element and the West or metal element. Her legs merge at the important acupoint CV-1, also known as Metal Gate. This is the Northwest Gate, alternatively known as the Mysterious Pass. Representing a state between nonbeing (zero) and being (one) it is the doorway to the state of the golden secret of all life.[6] Lao Tzu explained that this gateway provides access to the infinite intelligence of the Universe. He wrote in the *Tao de Jing* 'The Spirit of the Valley never dies. Hence comes the name Mysterious Female'. The two mountains in the background of the Temperance card create a valley in the center. Similar to the legs of a woman giving birth, they represent the female in Lao Tzu's quote. Applied to the body, the feminine valley floor would again depict the important acupoint between the legs, the first acupoint along the yin oriented Conception Vessel or CV-1. The solar crown being birthed in the scene is a symbol of the Great Mystery, arising through the feminine, which never dies.

In ancient Egyptian temples, the female sky goddess, Nut, arches her body through the sky. Touching the ground, she connects with the earth god, Geb, through her feet and hands. Together *yin* and *yang* unite to form the Ouroborus symbol and the microcosmic orbit. The goddess Nut is the creative potential of *yin* Spirit and represents the Conception Vessel. Looking at the goddess Nut's figure independently, we see her swallowing the sun at sunset and rebirthing it at dawn. The sun travels through the center of her body in what the Chinese call the Central Channel. The winged solar disk or scarab beetle often pictured emerging from between Nut's legs are Egyptian symbols of Resurrection. We are shown through these images that there is great potential for renewal by refining the energy of body. Letting go of old perceptions of being less and separate from God within our cells, we awaken ultimately to our innate wholeness and perfection. Through an experience similar to

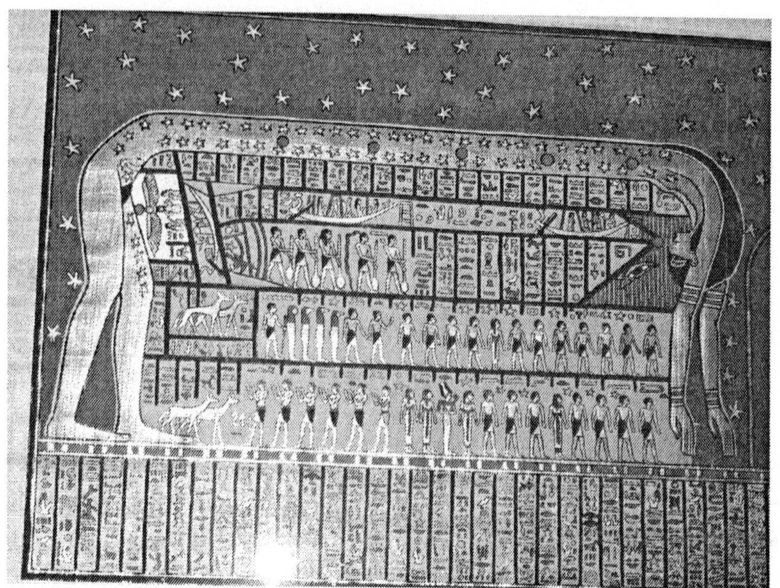

Papyrus painting of Egyptian goddess Nut forming the Ouroborus shape with her body. The passage of the sun can be seen going through her Central Channel.

labor cramps, spontaneous vibrations arising at CV-1 help release our concepts of less and eventually resurrect Christ consciousness within.

The solar image in the card appears as a golden crown. Likewise, in the symbolism of the Jewish Kabala, the crown is known as *Kether* and highlights the sacred marriage or God united with his female aspect *Shekina*.[2] Similarly, the Greek god Hermes gained his crown of wisdom and birthed the androgynous Hermaphroditus when uniting with the goddess of love, Aphrodite.[2] This crown at the top of the head is the raw fire and light of God. It is the location of the seventh and final chakra called *Sahasrana* where an individual becomes enlightened. *Sahasrana* is sometimes described as a mini vortex much like the whirling emptiness of central *qi* leading to the Tao.[29] No wonder the crown of the Temperance card is depicted at an angle to show us its circular shape. Once again the tarot highlights that wholeness is associated with the Ouroborus symbol.

The balanced offspring of the god Hermes and the goddess Aphrodite is an androgenous individual named Hermaphroditus.

Our ability to transform ourselves is achieved through the internal alchemical blending of the elements of fire (*yang*) and water (*yin*) within the lower *dan tian*. In the Temperance card, the blending and tempering of the different polarities within the golden vessels occurs in front of the lower *dan tian,* suggesting some significance. The fire element of *shen* Spirit ignites the water or *jing* essence of the body and causes it to vibrate and move. This synergy of opposites transmutes and refines the baser substance of *jing* essence into high vibrational *ling* creative spiritual potential. The golden goblets held by the angel suggest that the alchemical works can produce the human Holy Grail, another name for the immortal golden body.

The Chinese character for *jing* depicts grains of rice growing within an alchemical pot of cinnabar.[12] As the sun encourages the plants to grow in spring, so too can the sunshine of the eternal flow through the unrestricted Central Channel to unlock and awaken our potential within the lower *dan tian*. Qigong inner cultivation is an alchemical process that activates the transcendental force of the spiral known as central *qi*. The

Golden goblet from Ankara Museum in Turkey. According to legend only by acknowledging the dream experience and asking the right questions will a questing individual find the elusive Holy Grail to restore health and prosperity to the land.

alchemical pot, as metaphor for the lower *dan tian*, is the place to purify the *yin* soul. Rising upwards, the *yin* soul of the metal element merges with the *yang* soul of the wood element. Yin metal begets yang wood. Enhancing the physical body we nourish our spiritualized nature as symbolized by the growth of plants in the card.

What is our full potential? From a Chinese Taoist perspective, we build and refine the energies of our bodies through Qigong for long health, longevity, peace of mind and wisdom. However, the greatest achievement of the spiritual adept is the cultivation of the immutable immortal golden body. As a means of transcending the boundaries of time, one can enter the golden gates of heaven by developing what is symbolized in the Temperance card as the blooming of flowers, particularly golden irises. The 'Yellow Flower' is an alternate name for the golden immortal body. Also known as the 'Mysterious Embryo,'[20] we see again the significance of the angel mixing the elixir of life in front of the womb, the location of the lower *dan tian* and our inner creative development.

Description of how to do Spiral Qigong

Keeping your mind's eye deep within the earth, feel or imagine the energies blending, churning and swirling. Follow the movements with your hands if you like. This gentle blending of heavenly and earthly energies is the alchemical blending of *yang* and *yin,* fire and water. Allow the potential energy to build until the energies shift and begin spiraling upwards in a counter-clockwise direction through and around the body.

Chapter 6

The Sun

> Catholic churches in South America often depict the cross of Christ wrapped in a cloth that spirals upwards in a counter-clockwise direction. Celtic crosses sometimes depict Christ as a central spiral.

In the previous card, the background image shows the newly born sun. Here in the Sun card, we have the image of the solar *yang* principle, highlighted and expressed thrice: through the image of the sun in the sky, the Son of humanity (with a golden Ouroborus crown upon the head) and the sunflowers of the earth. This *yang* depiction in the three worlds represents the heavenly influence within the three *dan tian* of the body. The *I Ching* explains the cyclical aspect of the universe and human nature by the use of three horizontal lines called trigrams. These lines represent the upper, middle and lower worlds. When the lines are solid they represent *yang* while the broken lines depict *yin*. The placement of three *yang* or unbroken lines together creates the trigram called the sky. Representing this trigram, the Sun card is a symbol for strength and the divine power of the infinite; the divine child as the golden embryo fully knows him or herself. Living in the physical plane of the immanent, the immortal body is connected with Source through the red feather rising upwards upon his head. Holding a red spiraling banner, the immortal body is linked to the rise of the central *qi* that unites all of existence as one.

We can gain insight into the horse symbolism on this card by exploring the history of Indian religious practices. The horse sacrifice (*as'vamedha)* was a most revered and celebrated ritual in the Vedic tradition of India. Of Indo European origin, there are also traces of horse sacrifice in German, Greek, Roman, Armenian and Iranian cultural backgrounds.[27] In India, the horse sacrifice became a major religious rite of renewal for the victorious King.[27] The horse, often synonymous with the symbol of the serpent (some say because it holds the antidote to snake venom), is a metaphor for the cosmos. The act of bloodletting and sacrifice performed by men replaced the sacred menstruating rituals of peaceful matriarchal societies.[23] The blood sacrifice was (and in some cultures continues to be) likewise believed to be a ritual action to cleanse, purify and regenerate the heavens as well as the physical world.

Kings, as mediators between heaven and earth, had the responsibility of maintaining order, abundance and fertility in the land. The aging sovereign was in earlier times killed through sacrifice to regenerate royal power and maintain fertility in agriculture based societies.[27] However, at some point the horse became a symbolic substitute or scapegoat for the King. Through the animal's death, the King experienced a mythical rebirth and became one with the immortal gods.[27]

The Drink of Victory (*Vaja peya*) was a ceremonial race between seventeen horses. During the race, the King and Queen climbed the sacred post, ascending to the sun.[27] This appears to be a ritual reenactment of the rising central *qi* within the central axis of the body when masculine (*yang*) and feminine (*yin*) energies unite together. There are also similarities to the Incan sacred hitching post of the sun and the Maypole spiral dance marking the return or rebirth of spring in Europe.

The Brahman literature of 1000 to 800 BCE explained another reason for the sacrifice from a cosmologic standpoint. In the beginning, the original one, *Prajapati,* was unmanifested totality as symbolized by a cosmic egg. He 'heated' himself to create and populate the earth, heavens and humans.[27] This act of creation was exhausting and loosened the joints of his cosmic body.

Unable to rise on his own accord, his healing occurred through the ritual of *agnihotra,* the building of the sacrificial fire alter. During the ritual process, the priests restored *Prajapati* and the cosmos back to their original oneness through the laying of bricks to form the altar of fire.[27]

Go back further in history to the Neolithic era and we have the cosmic egg within the womb of the goddess. Representing the undifferentiated oneness of our origins it was through the act of giving birth that time began and all that is physical in the universe was created. This is why so many of the earliest clay figurines at archeological sites emphasize the beauty of a well rounded belly in female form. This was to highlight the creative potential of the physical body within the lower abdomen. This source of fertility and abundance is what the inner traditions of Chinese Medicine refer to as the elixir field of the lower *dan tian.* And when we heat up and transform the subconscious in the symbolic underworld, we embrace the feminine potency of working with the body. Qigong inner cultivation techniques can then help unlock and restore the spiritual force within ourselves and the earth.

> Some Paleolithic goddess deities emphasize a cosmic egg within a large lower abdomen. The egg represents the oneness of the Tao in ancient China.

In the Sun card, the horse and bricks depict the sacrifice of ego leading to spiritual rebirth through the growing flowers and the youth's floral crown. The Hindu gods themselves were once mortal, achieving their immortality and divinity through the sacrifice. The idea developed that through blood and sacrifice, anyone was capable of developing a spiritual and indestructible part of themselves.[27] Upon physical death, the individual now deified or immortal could return to the timeless and eternal existence.

Animal sacrifice later gave way to individual aesthetic techniques of internal 'heating' in the East. The popular sun salute of *hatha* yoga likely has its roots in the earlier sacrificial religious rite explained above. The word *hatha* derives from *ha* meaning sun and *tha* meaning moon.[5] *Hatha* yoga is an Eastern cultivation technique bringing union to the pair of opposites. Similarly, Qigong practitioners reunite feminine and masculine principles back into the transcendental Tao. Through inner alchemy they can heat and purify the body and mind. Working to revitalize the womb-like lower *dan tian,* Qigong connects with and nourishes the cosmic egg of our beginnings within.

Description of how to do Spiral Qigong

Allow the central *qi* to whirl and blend with the energies of your body. Do not try to direct the flow of energy to any particular location; just allow it to guide your whole being. Begin to move and express your body consciousness through movement.

Spontaneous movements can be slow or quick, subtle or obvious, gentle or strong. If you feel an inclination to move in a certain way or change position, follow that prompting. Qigong movement meditation can be done in any position. Options include standing, sitting, walking or lying on the ground. Allow the body to move into stillness as it wishes. Trust your natural instincts.

Chapter 7

The Empress

Jing essence is the most *yin* energy in the body. A plentiful supply is desirable and leads to physical health. Someone with an abundance of *jing* essence feels strong and has great endurance. He or she exudes a natural vitality in body and strong mind while maintaining a positive attitude towards life. As a bonus, individuals with healthy *jing* maintain a youthful appearance, also experiencing greater sexual and creative potency. In Chinese Medicine theory, essence is slowly depleted as we age. It is also unnaturally lost through overwork or unhealthy emotional strain. The depletion of essence which corresponds to the aging process is, however, reduced by maintaining a balanced lifestyle with quiet times for meditation. Meditation of any kind is also a great way to slow down and reconnect with the self by letting the body and mind naturally synchronize.

Jing essence can be regenerated through inner cultivation techniques such as Qigong. Regular practice is known to halt or slow down signs of aging. Qigong is an easy to learn exercise to improve health and prevent disease in the first place. The basic method for achieving health and long life comes from building and refining this *jing* sexual energy in the lower *dan tian* of the belly.[7] Concluding Qigong practice, we always want to finish by guiding the energies we have generated from our practice into the storehouse of the lower *dan tian*. Like a reservoir, the energy contained in this center can replenish the other energy channels, ultimately providing nourishment to the internal organs, bones, muscles, connective tissue, skin and brain of the physical body.

Inherited from our parents, our essence is determined at conception via the union of the egg of the mother and the sperm of the father. *Jing,* therefore, connects us to our ancestral past and our genetic history. It is associated with the element of water and the fluids of the body. Related to the kidneys and adrenals, the water element is responsible for physical growth, development and reproduction. Healthy essence is also critical for relaxation, renewal and rejuvenation of the body. Water corresponds with the season of winter, the darkness of night and the direction of the North. It is the dark blue or blackness of the deep sea. As the element closest to the Tao, water represents the introspective awareness necessary for receiving guidance from the Dreamtime and the collective unconscious. This is one reason why Qigong, with focus on building *jing* essence in the lower *dan tian,* is such an effective means to enhance dreaming.

The celestial animal of the water element is the warrior tortoise. This animal is noted for great longevity and a strong immune system. Moving slowly and gently like the turtle, we can learn from this animal's wisdom and maintain a healthy supply of essence. The celestial turtle of the North is also encircled by a serpent. Here we have the association of the Ouroborus and the microcosmic orbit with the North. It is the spiral that transforms and enlightens our physical, emotional, mental and spiritual nature. Being a warrior reflects the ability of the *jing* essence to help the body ward off and be unaffected by external influences and disease.

In the Empress card, we find the Queen lounging on her low-lying throne. She rests and rejuvenates upon pillows and a blanket of red. The central *qi,* depicted as the red color of the cinnabar field, has risen from below the earth and strengthened the energy supply of *jing* essence in the lower *dan tian.* The abundance of sexual energy in the lower *dan tian* is shown by the cylindrical red pillow encircled by a golden band near the Empress' lower abdomen. The golden Ouroborus shape shows the fullness of essence within the lower *dan tian.* From the alchemical synergy of fire and water, *jing* has been warmed and transmuted into *ling* spiritual potency. Central *qi* now continues to rise upwards like steam returning *ling* to its noble position at the heart center in the middle *dan tian*. Note that in the Empress card the throne itself is heart-shaped and includes the symbol of Venus and the feminine gender. The red pillows, likewise, rise upwards to include yet not surpass the chest cavity, the area governed by the middle elixir field.

The Empress is the *yin* aspect of the divinity known as *ling* Spirit. The downward flow of blessings from heaven associated with the Chinese character for *ling* appears as water cascading downward from a garden of paradise in the background of the card. Below the feet of the Empress, we see fertility represented by the young growth of golden wheat. As a substitute for rice in the jing Chinese character, the sprouting of new vegetation, nonetheless, shows spiritual rewards from physical transmutation. With regular Qigong practice, we build spiritual potency.

This goddess figurine from the Neolithic archeological site at Catal Hoyuk, Turkey rests upon a low lying throne flanked by lions. It was found in a grain bin marking another symbolic association with the

Waite Empress card where the growing of wheat is depicted. There have been no signs of war or violence found by archeologists at the site. Spiral artifacts and other symbolic artwork show these early people were connected with and honored the mythical dimension of life. Perhaps the remains of their culture model our own potential for peace and the development of virtues through dreaming.

Then we, like the Empress in this card, hold within ourselves the golden scepter of power to help restore order and harmony to the land.

With her head among the stars, the Empress is connected to the heavens as well as the earth. She is a channel for the omnipotence of Spirit. The development of *ling yin* Spirit is critical to the alchemical process of refining the body's energies. The deepest and most hidden pillow behind the Empress is the color black of the *yin* watery element. Decorated with *ankhs,* the Egyptian symbol for eternal life, the card hints at the promise of spiritual rebirth coming into being.

Author dreams of Mother Mary with her head encircled by a halo of stars.

Description of how to do Spiral Qigong

When you are ready to conclude, slow down your movements until your body comes to a rest. Gently place both hands on the lower abdomen. The left hand goes on top for women and the right hand on top for men for the perfect *yin yang* balance. With eyes still closed, take a few deep breaths grounding the energies you have generated, the fruits of your Qigong practice, deeply into your lower *dan tian*. When you feel the energy is stable and condensed into the smallest of spheres within the center of the pelvic girdle, slowly open your eyes.

> Egyptian hieroglyphs of serpents rising are common in ancient temples. Some are shown lifting up the sun, symbol of spiritual illumination. Serpent hieroglyphs are also often found with the ankh, an Egyptian symbol of eternal life.

Chapter 8

The Emperor

According to the religious scholar Mircea Eliade, it was during the age of shamanism that techniques for internal heating were mastered and most prevalent. The ancient Chinese shamans and enlightened ones, called *wu*, channeled the wisdom and power of 'the Great One' on Earth primarily through dance, song, music making and synchronizing with nature in what is known as shamanic Qigong. As healers, rainmakers, mediums and soul travelers, the *wu* were able to travel into different dimensions of reality in the dream state.[5] Body minded spiritual practices were fundamental for the health and spiritual development of the Taoists and Priest Kings who followed. Referred to as the 'Dragon' and 'the first born son of heaven', the most revered of the five dominant Dragon Kings during China's Golden Age was Huang Ti. Associated with the color yellow, he represented the central earth element that stabilizes the other directions.[5] Legend tells that Huang Ti was conceived when a golden ray of light emanating from heaven entered the womb of his Mother. Having a dragon-like appearance and wisdom beyond his years, he later became one of the most influential founders of Chinese Medicine.[5] Huang Ti recorded jewels of wisdom and inner cultivation techniques for maintaining health and longevity in *The Chinese Classic of the Yellow Emperor*, a text often referenced in the study of Oriental Medicine today. Taoist myth states that the Yellow Emperor distilled the elixir of life and immortality within a golden cauldron and lived up to 111 years. Upon his death, he transcended the human experience riding a dragon to heaven. He flew to the Realm of the Immortals in his etheric and immutable dragon body,[5] another name for the spiritualized immortal body.

> At the base of the Apprentice Pillar in Roslyn Chapel in Scotland are eight dragons. The vines emerging from their mouths spiral up the pillar in a counterclockwise direction, the same direction and movement of the transcendental central qi associated with the wood element and created during Spiral Qigong. Knights Templar's believed the Holy Grail could be found within the Pillar. Qigong cultivates the personal Holy Grail of the practitioner.

Within Paradise, Huang Ti enjoys a blissful, timeless existence among the blessed.[20]

Lao Tzu explained that through a state of emptiness, knowledge of self and universe arise intuitively from the infinite intelligence. Exploring our inner world, internal experiences surface naturally as words and visual images when our minds are relaxed and stable. The symbolic and literal promptings of the dream state helps us understand the natural course or action to take.

Living in the Tao is comparable to flowing down stream as it is a natural, calm and effortless action. Acting against inner knowledge alternatively is difficult, like swimming against a strong current. When we are working hard without making any progress, it is best to assess how to get back on track and be in harmony with our true selves. Opposing the Tao can lead to overexertion, depression, anxiety and disease. Lao Tzu stated that it was also the source of karma.[6] Similarly, the Catholic Church defines hell as the self created illusion or separation from God.[2] To find true bliss and happiness, we must have the confidence and wisdom to act authentically on our inner intuitive promptings even when they contradict the status quo. Going with the flow is the way to prosperity and wellness. Following the will of heaven, we can only act appropriately.

The Emperor as mediator between heaven and earth aligns

himself with divine will to maintain harmony in his kingdom through appropriate action. The Emperor card shows the King's connection with *shen* Spirit and the element of fire that resides in the heart through his red attire and the heart shaped image upon his left shoulder. Having a white beard and rams heads as an emblem on his stately tall throne, he exhibits an abundance of strong mental and spiritual *yang* or masculine energy appropriate to his royal position of leadership. The spiral horns above his head show that central *qi* has risen throughout the body awakening the whole Central Channel and the Trinity within.

> Helping Jason in his quest for the Golden Fleece Medea transforms an old ram into a youthful one within her magic cauldron in a story associated with the Greek Mysteries. Regenerative cauldrons (symbolic of the lower dan tian) are also associated with the womb of the Great Goddess in Celtic and Norse traditions.

The fiery colored background, along with the dry mountain landscape, emphasize the *yang* or masculine quality of this card. The Emperor holds an elongated Egyptian *Shenring* (zero and one together) in his right hand representing eternity.[29] The golden Ouroborus at its pinnacle shows the abundance of spiritual energy within the upper *dan tian* of the head. Depicted as a hollow or empty golden ring, the alchemical marriage between the self and Tao has been achieved. The golden orb in the Emperor's left hand is a symbol of cosmic order where *shen ling* union is achieved.[30] Hands are instruments for working in this world – they are how we primarily interact with the physical universe we live in. They are also the primary instrument of the body for external Qigong healing through the acupoint Lao Gong in the center of the palms. The Emperor's worldly influence is in harmony with the Tao as seen by the throne's spiraling horns near his hands. Holding the golden orb he consciously channels the harmonizing influence of central *qi* into the physical plane. This is how any child of heaven helps maintains peace and prosperity in his or her kingdom. Working to clear the Central Channel, the tarot teaches that we can each be a unifying force in our world.

Upon the Emperor's head rests a golden crown fixed with red and blue gems that match his red over blue costume. Often depicted in similar reds and blues are the Virgin Mary and Jesus Christ of medieval Christianity and the Shiva with Shakti of Hinduism and Tibetan Buddhism.[28] Red represents the enlivened color of the blood (or awakened cinnabar field of the Central Channel) while blue represents the color of spiritualized matter.[28] This dark blue or indigo color is also the color associated with the sixth chakra or third eye in the Hindu and Tantric systems. Representing spiritual vision, it reflects the Emperor's ability to have conscious understanding of the nature of the Tao.

Christianity adopted the serpent swallower symbol of the Ouroborus to explain the limitations of the material existence that is the cause of suffering in the world. The cyclical serpent body helps connect us symbolically with nature's seasonal rhythms and tune into our own cycles of the soul. In Qigong, we harmonize with the seasons and the elements of life. Being fluid throughout life's changes, we prevent ourselves from becoming stuck and out of synchronicity with the harmony of the universe. Flowing through cycles of birth, growth, death and rebirth, we ultimately gain personal experience and knowledge into the timeless oneness behind material existence. Having cleared our sense of separation, we see through the now transparent veils of illusion. Centered within the emptiness of the Ouroborus circle, we remain peaceful, and a positive influence through our thoughts and actions, despite the apparent woes of the world.

The story goes that Athena, the Greek goddess of wisdom, had an unusual birth. While in the womb of her mother Metis, a prophecy was made that the child born would overthrow her father Zeus. Zeus, hearing these words, feared being dethroned and he swallowed up (transforming the physical into spiritual) the unsuspecting Metis.[20] Later, Zeus began having awful migraine headaches. His son, Hephaestus, was the blacksmith amongst the gods (alchemical metal worker). He responded to Zeus's cries of pain by cutting open the top of Zeus's head with an ax. Out from the cranial opening (GV-20) sprang Athena, fully grown and armored in a spiritual rebirth of consciousness. Brandishing her lance (Central Channel) and giving a war cry (divine energetic expression), she proclaimed, like the Buddha had, her authentic nature to the world. In so doing, Athena demonstrated her strength and ability to face and abolish all fears.

A popular protective goddess of Oriental origin, Athena, like the Queen of the West, came to the timely assistance of many a hero. Helping Heracles complete his labors, she later guided him to heaven where she placed him among the stars. Athena also helped Odysseus through his challenges following the Trojan War, facilitating his spiritual journey home in ten years – one and zero combined. Remaining ever virginal (state of purified body) and quick of mind and action, Athena is a symbol of divine knowledge and transcendental wisdom. She teaches, in the words of Lao Tzu, 'confidence in the consistency and hence the intelligibility, of the world.'[6] Her birth continues to be celebrated annually in Greece by the Festival of the Golden Rain. Through her symbolic birth she brought the golden manna, the ambrosia of immortality, from heaven to earth.[31] Athena's story demonstrates spiritual wisdom obtained through the rise of the awakened central *qi*.

Description of how to do Spiral Qigong

Upon completion of the Qigong exercise, take out your journal and record your internal experiences while you were practicing Qigong. Describe any images, feelings, words, tactile sensations, aha's or smells experienced. If you are interested in going deeper into the dream state of your experience, try drawing or painting as a means of enhancing conscious recall. You could alternately pick a tarot card and see what messages from the divine come through the symbols you see and the images that hold your attention. Assess the meaning and message of any insights as you would a dream, determining how best to apply their guidance in your life. Other dreams and synchronicities may follow in the days ahead and should also be included in your journal to help see the overall pattern and messages of your inner guidance system.

Be thankful for this time to reconnect with yourself through Qigong. Intend to carry the benefits of Qigong practice in the days and weeks ahead, letting your authentic nature shine.

Cautionary Note: In spontaneous Qigong, it is important to allow the energies to flow naturally and to not let the limited ego mind run the show. Forcing energies to move up the spine or intentionally contracting CV-1, for example, may not be in your best interest and could cause negative effects such as overriding the bioelectrical system of the body. Listen and recognize when your body has had enough. It may be only a few minutes or a few seconds but the practice is potent nonetheless. Stop and rest if uncomfortable symptoms such as dizziness, headache or nausea arise. Note that the body could need time to assimilate higher frequencies of energy coming in.

If feelings of physical or emotional discomfort present themselves afterwards, the symptoms may reflect a healing crisis showing where long term issues or emotions have been stuck and stored internally. Symptoms may be coming into conscious awareness and therefore experienced for the first time. However, always check with a doctor if there are any symptoms of concern. If symptoms are subclinical (not reflective of a health issue) Qigong students can consider additional body oriented energy modalities such as acupuncture, herbal medicine, shiatsu Japanese bodywork, homeopathy, craniosacral therapy, reflexology, massage, homeopathy and Reiki in addition to Qigong practice to facilitate the clearing of the issue at hand.

Part III: Tarot Dreaming

Section A: The Virtues of *Yin*

Chapter 9

The Wheel of Fortune

In 1998, I was a reservist in the Coast Guard and a young mother of two young children, ages three and one. My husband's job had moved us back to the Northwest and we had driven to the coast to spend time with his family during the Thanksgiving holiday. It was early in the morning following Thanksgiving Day and while everyone else slumbered, I lay awake in the dark. Looking for a distraction, I picked up a book my mom had been urging me to read. Mom thought the section on anger would help me get in touch with suppressed emotions regarding my parents' divorce over a decade earlier. Skeptical that I even had any anger about the situation, I skimmed through the small chapter all the same. Unaffected and unimpressed, I nonetheless looked in the table of contents for another section to peruse. I found a chapter on fears and feeling mildly curious, I began reading, though I did not have high expectations. The reading, however, soon captivated my attention. Though I felt quite happy in my marriage and home life, I realized as I read that there were important interests I had not pursued; that, in effect, I was letting my fears get the best of me. I had always considered myself to be brave and independent having grown up an only child and a latch key kid. How could I be fearful? After all, I had left my family to live and study abroad during high school and loved to push through the boundaries of things that scared me with extreme sports. Perhaps that was why I was taken aback. I was confronted with an entirely different form of fear.

As I read I began to recall memories when I had let fears override what I wanted to do: I yearned to try out for the high school play, yet snuck away before the audition began. The fear of failure, the risk of embarrassing myself in front of others and the thought that I might not be good enough stopped me back then from even trying. Moreover, it was in high school that I shifted away from fun art classes. Deciding to be a serious student, I instead focused on the science track in preparation for college and a future career in biology.

Closing the book I contemplated the many subtle ways I had suppressed my creative impulses. Gazing pensively forward in the dark, I had the following vision:

Dream 1: I see a youthful Native American woman in a white buckskin dress. She is beautiful with long flowing straight black hair. One hand is raised above her head, the other palm faces the ground. With eyes closed, she begins moving counterclockwise. Floating off the ground, she continues to spiral upward into the sky. As she ascends peacefully, I watch her long dark hair billowing gracefully in the wind behind her for several seconds. After several revolutions, the young woman transforms into an angel with large white wings before becoming pure and radiant white light.

The scene changes and I see the Native American woman now on the ground leaning on the earth with her right side and hand. Her back is towards me but she faces a middle aged Native American man who is sitting cross legged at the base of a tree gazing towards my direction. The dream scene focuses into a close up of the man at the tree. He speaks. 'Smiling Eyes, you need to do this.' Then, with a smile that shines through his eyes, he gazes lovingly up towards the sky. Moving his palms to his collarbones, he slowly and carefully extends his arms, lowering his hands palms up until they come to rest on his thighs.

I had this dream almost ten years ago. I did not really know anything about tarot cards then, but looking back I find that the woman's hand placement, connecting with earth below and heaven above, is like that of the Magician described in Part I. The woman in my dream also moved in a circular motion like the snake belt around his waist. The dream similarly shares components of the Fool card. The man at the tree is connected to the wood element and raises his head and chest skyward.

In retrospect dream 1 also shows the steps for doing Spiral Qigong, as described earlier in Part II. Bringing the energy downward through his arm movements the Native American man is bringing the energies of heaven down to earth as shown in the Hermit and Star cards. The upwards spiraling Native American woman represents the spiraling upward force of the central *qi* following the alchemical blending of yin and yang through the Sun, Empress and Emperor cards. Spiraling up into the sky the woman is transformed into an angel and then pure light, symbols of enlightenment and divine union.

This was my first recollected dream of a spiral. I did not yet know anything about Chinese Medicine, Qigong, shamanism, alchemy, or kundalini awakenings. Nor did I understand what the implications of this woman floating upwards in the whirling wind could be. I only knew that the dream validated the wisdom of earth-centered spiritual traditions, as represented by the Native American dream figures. I instinctively felt I had experienced a *big* dream and that it was important for me to explore the fuller meaning of the dreaming experience. From what I could make of the Native American man's movements, I was being directed to open my heart but how was I to do this? There seemed to be more behind the dream's message than simply repeating the arm movements I had seen. Having been renamed in the vision, I knew some sort of initiation had taken place within the Dreamtime and that somehow the earlier 'aha,' of consciously recognizing some of my own fears, had opened a space for spiritual insight to come through and guide me.

There is more to the story. Feeling thoroughly shell-shocked after the vision, I lay down next to my husband. Resting quietly in the fetal position with my right arm close to my chest, I felt the area over my heart thump outwards for an instant. I experienced the movement both inside my chest and against my arm. Although this was difficult to believe by the scientific standards of my education, I had experienced it and, therefore, could not rationally dismiss it. Within a few minutes of the chest movement, an uncomfortable achy sensation was noticeable within the left side of my chest. Something within my heart had begun to awaken, as old issues were consciously acknowledged. I had just palpably experienced the mind body connection. As though by divine arrangement, my mom, who had received Reiki energy training, was with us over the holiday and was available the next morning to give me a treatment. I noticed during this and subsequent treatments that the achy pain in my chest would subside, at least temporarily, when she put her hands on my body. How curious I became about how the bioenergetics of the body could lead to healing. I wanted the pain to go away, but I also wanted to learn more about energy healing. This 'opportunity' would propel me onward in a new creative direction. My interest in holistic health led me to study Traditional Chinese Medicine. This 3,000 year old Asian health care system had thoroughly mapped the energetic highways of the body and detailed different protocols for balancing the human energy system for health and wellness. The World Health Organization listed acupuncture as an effective treatment for over 250 medical conditions. Researchers in the United States were beginning to confirm the therapeutic efficacy of this Chinese modality for a variety of physical disorders as well as emotional stresses stored within the body.

It was during my studies in Oriental Medicine that I began taking Qigong classes; 45 minutes of Qigong practice twice a week really made a difference in my life. It put me in touch with my body and despite the hectic study load with school, I stayed calm and focused. When the whole family caught the stomach flu, my immune system stayed strong despite caretaking to everyone for a couple evenings and studying for finals. I remained healthy and vital then and throughout the years of my training. I was also experiencing some vivid dreams and beneficial synchronistic events. I knew Qigong practice was good for me on many different levels.

Many years later as a practicing acupuncturist I was intuitively led to use Spiral Qigong to maintain a healthy lifestyle. Unexpectedly, my dreaming deepened and reached new levels. Dream recall improved with heightened spiritual communications coming through. With only 5-30 minutes of Spiral Qigong practice a week, sacred symbols and spiritual beings from different ancient cultures around the world appeared in dreams on a daily basis. This happened primarily while sleeping, lying awake in bed in the mornings and during or after Qigong sessions. With increasing frequency, my dreams showed a progression of spiritual development. More and more I dreamed of the symbols on the different tarot cards or would visually watch as the cards themselves appeared from out of thin air. Recording the dreams in my dream journal, I would later research their mysterious meanings in my waking life. It was as though I was given little pieces of a puzzle that over time showed a pattern I could interpret. Putting the pieces together I realized the inherent Asian symbolism of the cards and the Tao of tarot connection. My individualized spiritual experience showed itself to be of universal significance. Initiated through the practice of Qigong and consciously understood through dream analysis, the two showed themselves to be intricately linked in what I refer to as Qigong Dreaming. Qigong Dreaming has transformed me. The result of my inner explorations is the creation of this book.

The first series of dreams focused on water. Over and over again, I would see water pouring downward and collecting in different bowls or vases. The containers varied but the general theme remained the same. The overall quality of the vase itself seemed to develop and refine over time. Initial dreams of clay bowls were later replace by glass or crystal vases. The patterns and pictures upon the vases also seemed to become more intricate and elaborate over time.

One of the main goals of Qigong is to strengthen the physical energy center of the body in the lower abdomen. This area, the lower *dan tian,* is likened to a cup or small container. Resting in the middle of the pelvic cavity, it is a reservoir for *jing* essence. *Jing* is the most material form of energy in the body and is related to the element of water. With regular Qigong practice, the storehouse of physical *jing* energy strengthens as well. My water dreams were depicting the building of essence in the lower *dan tian* occurring through Spiral Qigong practice. As the quantity of *jing* increased within me so too did the size and the evolution of the vessels collecting water in my dreams.

The following dream marked another step in my development:

> *Dream 2: I see a large clear crystal vase resting on the ground. Two thin streams of water begin flowing upwards out of the top of the vase spinning counterclockwise opposite each other in a coordinated movement.*

Spiral Qigong is different to the spontaneous Qigong forms I have previously tried. Rather than focusing on bringing the energies down into the lower *dan tian* it emphasizes guiding the energies further down through the lower half of the Central Channel and into the earth. Blending the energies of heaven and earth within the earth is what creates the harmonious and powerful central *qi*. I and many of my students have had a sense of the spiral energy suddenly forming and rising upwards as they practice this form of Qigong. Compared by Taoists to a gentle mist rising or a whirling vortex, the transcendental central *qi* builds and transforms *jing* essence into *ling* spiritual potency. Once the energies of the lower *dan tian* reach a certain threshold, they begin to naturally rise to awaken the middle and upper *dan tian*, the emotional and spiritual centers of the body, respectively.

Author with lizard ouroborus fountain in Yallingup, Western Australia. A larger version of the Holy Grail the fountain of youth brings renewal and youthful appearance to those who drink from it. Qigong with its emphasis on building life force energy in the body is thought to do the same thing.

Dragons are associated with moving water in China. The upward moving snake-like streams of water in dream 2 reflected the now ascending energies of the sacred serpent spiral and *ling* spiritual power. Other dreams of this central *qi* rising would include snakes, pasta tubes, hoses, electrical pulsations, dust, steam and smoke spiraling upwards to signify the same process.

Spiritual awakening happens most often in small steps and stages. The psyche knows when the student is ready for advancement to the next level. As Dream 1 illustrates, enlightenment can occur with a sudden 'aha' or insight gained whether from dream analysis, the reflection of a learning experience, an encounter with another person or simply reading a passage in a book that has significant impact. It can also be intentionally cultivated by doing internal practices such as Spiral Qigong which purify the body so it can assimilate higher frequency energies or using Qigong Dreaming techniques. Awakening to enlightenment is a natural process and includes anything that helps us grow and become more authentic.

Looking at the Wheel of Fortune, we see the red spiral as the central image of this card. The counterclockwise movement appears to be initiated by the movement of the red dog-headed figure in the bottom right hand corner. Here Anubis, the guardian of the Underworld, in turning the wheel, is turning back the clock of time to clear the subconscious limitations of the past and negative emotions stored within the body. The sacred spiral of central *qi* is, therefore, helping the individual mature and grow as depicted by the four golden-winged figures in the card. They are reading and learning what Lao Tzu called virtues. As we clear and cleanse our destructive influences, we move from attracting low level experiences into manifesting abundance and wellness. Raising the consciousness of the body, positive experiences naturally flow and are attracted into the Qigong student's life. The path to harmonious existence with nature allows things to come into being, smoothly and effortlessly.

Spiral remain from the Temple of Cybele in modern day Turkey.

Author dreams of the Wheel of Fortune showing the Egyptian god Anubis sitting upon and spinning a counter-clockwise rotating line until it comes to rest in a horizontal position of balance.

The Anubis figure's ascent on the right side of the wheel represents the upward movement of

> Naga Kings at temple entrances in India show the Wheel of Fortune as a means to escape from the cycle of reincarnation and return to the central stillness of the transcendental. Reincarnation was an acceptable Christian belief prior to the Council of Nicea in 325 CE with salvation achievable by all through union with God.

the Governing Vessel along the spine. His spine is against the wheel to highlight this point. The golden serpent's descent on the left side of the wheel reflects the downward movement of the Conception Vessel. Note that the snake slithers along the front centerline of the body upon the wheel. Together these two figures complete the microcosmic orbit. *Yin* and *yang* are in balance within the self for health, wellness and spiritual illumination. The serpent in the image is golden in color. The immortal golden dragon body known to Taoists can be internally cultivated and realized by anyone actively using the revolving wheel or spiral of the Ouroborus. Once the golden body is perfected, the still point of God can be known as symbolized by the motionless celestial Sphinx. Soul united with Spirit, the world continues to turn but the individual retains a deep sense of peace and centeredness.

The headdress in black for *yin* and white for *yang* upon the Sphinx shows balance. The serpentine-shaped tail brings to mind ancient images of Hindu goddesses with cobras flowing out of the vaginal floor and rising upward. The Sphinx's tail connects with the central *qi* of the Wheel of Fortune spiral. The tail tucked underneath shows the closing off or contraction of the powerful acupoint CV-1 between the legs. Occurring naturally through spontaneous Qigong movement, the resulting vibrations help clear obstructions and channel in greater states of consciousness both through the microcosmic wheel and the Central Channel (depicted in the Wheel of Fortune card as the sword). The Sphinx's sword points to the open beak or mouth of the bird in the upper right hand corner. The mouth in Qigong is the upper

> Four intersecting lines forming a circle create the cryptic message in Greek meaning "Jesus Son of God" at Ephesus in Turkey. Eight lines also create the ba gua, a Chinese tool to restore harmony through feng shui and are common in indigenous artwork and medicine wheels around the world.

axis of the microcosmic orbit and the spiritual gate of the eternal Tao. The Sphinx's 'Mona Lisa' smile betrays her divine knowledge of both the physical and spiritual worlds. The wisdom of the Sphinx comes from the Tao. Her riddles when understood reveal the secrets of immortal life and the esoteric mysteries of the universe.

> Indigenous cultures throughout the Americas often walk or dance in a counterclockwise circle in ceremonies to access a dimension beyond time.

Chapter 10

The High Priestess

Dream 3: I see my maternal grandmother coming out of a hospital. Walking down a few steps, she crosses the street until she is standing right in front of me. Handing me a red hair band she insists 'It's important you start with the crane. You need to start with the crane.

At the time of the dream, I was contemplating two different Chinese Medicine Qigong programs and unsure which to pursue. One of the schools, the Oregon College of Oriental Medicine (OCOM), offered a four year study of Oriental Medicine while the other program focused solely on Qigong training. Soaring Crane Qigong was part of the first year curriculum at OCOM. Dream 3 came as guidance and helped direct me to the right school and training. The dream also conveyed a deeper prophetic meaning, though I didn't recognize the significance of where Qigong would lead me until many years later.

In this dream, my mother's mother is the Priestess. Coming from my maternal ancestral lineage, she also represents the *yin jing* essence of the lower *dan tian*. This sexual and creative energy of the body governs physical health in Chinese theory. It is associated with the energies of the moon and water as seen in the High Priestess card.

Coming out of a hospital, my grandmother, as an older and wiser aspect of myself, is a messenger of healing. Her descent of the stairs represents the stepping down of awareness of the infinite intelligence of the universe from the upper heavens to the world of physical existence. Crossing the street, my grandmother passes through a threshold or gateway (*xuan*) into the collective unconscious. Through internal stillness (*wu*) and inner awareness (*you*) of nighttime dreaming, I was receptive to the divine guidance from the Dreamtime.

In my dream, the red circular hair band is a metaphor for the Tao. I use hair bands to put my hair in a ponytail at the top of my head before I go to sleep. The red circular shape is a metaphor for the dragon Ouroborus. Through Qigong, I will awaken the red elixir field for health and wellness. As a hair band at the crown of the head, the dream signifies that wisdom and spiritual illumination are a potential reality. By starting with Soaring Crane Qigong, I will ultimately discover a tool for spiritual transcendence.

Partially concealed within her cloak, the High Priestess holds within her hands a white spiraled document symbolizing the central *qi* of whirling emptiness within the Central Channel. It is quite similar to the white hollow tube belonging to the Queen of the West discussed earlier. Sitting between black and white, *yin* and *yang*, stone metal pillars, the High Priestess has entered the doorway to the collective unconscious. This is what Lao Tzu referred to as the means to the golden secret of all life. The Priestess' left hand and the lower corner of the document subtly point down towards acupoint CV-1. CV-1 is a physical threshold to initiate tremendous healing. Helping clear and cleanse the subconscious body, the Central Channel can channel in the vibrational signature of Source, represented by the word 'Tora' on the white scroll. Becoming clear and empty like the watery background of the card, the Central Channel, like a mirror, reflects the truth of heaven in the inner experience of the individual. We all contain the archetypal energy of the High Priestess and can be receptive to the wisdom of God.

Dream 4: During a Native American vision quest, I sat in isolation without food or water in 100+ weather for two and a half days. After two days of spiritual purging, I danced in celebration in my 9x9 foot questing space and fell to my knees exhausted by my exertion. Coming to rest upon the ground, my hips began unconsciously vibrating and moving on their own accord. My legs stretched out behind me and I began flexing my neck and spine low to the ground. Moving side to side, I realized my body was slithering on the earth like a snake. Fascinated, yet mentally detached from the situation, I watched as my serpentine body moved around in sensuous delight in a circle upon the ground. Completing one revolution, my body coiled inward into a tight ball, then suddenly struck outwards as though capturing some invisible prey before the movements stopped completely.

Soaring Crane Qigong training included learning a spontaneous standing form of Qigong. Rather than follow a prescribed format or routine, the body is instead encouraged to move on its own accord. Considered an advanced form of Qigong, spontaneous Qigong is recognized for its powerful healing abilities. Professor Hui Xian Chen, who brought Soaring Crane Qigong to the United States following guidance given to her by Jesus in a dream. She attributes her dedicated practice of this Qigong form to her full recovery from terminal breast cancer. Whether to address serious health issues, maintain wellness, or unlock spiritual dreaming, spontaneous Qigong is a powerful way to harness the powers of the conscious and unconscious mind.

In this last dreaming experience, it was solitary time in nature without food or water that helped awaken in me a nonlocal consciousness of dreaming. The Ouroborus was passed to me in Dream 3 as a hair band. In Dream 4, I expressed the revolving serpent through the spontaneous expression of my body movements. Going around in a circle upon the ground, I created the Ouroborus form. Striking out at the location where I had started emphasized the importance of the mouth with tail self-devouring imagery. Transforming the limitations of the physical through Qigong is similar to the digestion or internal combustion of food. Through symbolic death, the body becomes alchemically transmuted or enlivened into spiritualized matter – something to think about when we have dream figures being eaten and consumed.

The mouth and tail of the dragon Ouroborus are transition points between *yang* and *yin* in the body. The mouth as the upper point is connected to the heavens and *yang* in nature. The tail as the lower point closest to the earth is more *yin* from a Chinese perspective. One could also say that the mouth forms a zero shape and the tail that of a one. Between *yin* and *yang*, or zero and one, we have the gateway to the golden secret to all life. The mouth to tail connection marks a transitional opening to access universal knowledge.

Within the energetic meridian system of Chinese Medicine, transition points between the Conception Vessel and the Governing Vessel occur twice within the microcosmic orbit: at the tail end of the body on the perineum at acupoint CV-1 and within the mouth where the tongue rests upon the upper palate. These two locations are potent points for accessing high consciousness energies for powerful healing and dreaming.

Mystical times between *yin* and *yang* are known and celebrated by earth centered cultures. These transitional gateways include autumn and spring equinoxes and dusk and dawn. As a balance between opposing forces of nature, they provide a threshold for actively accessing the Dreamtime or working with conscious dreaming.

The Egyptian headdress on the High Priestess shows the eclipse or unity of sun and moon. Above her spiritual crown, *yang* and *yin* together return to eternal oneness above GV-20. The High Priestess is depicted in the card as quiet, calm and hidden beneath her attire. She represents the *yin* or feminine esoteric qualities of the divine, the inner awareness of the infinite and the intuitiveness of sacred dream incubation.

The High Priestess card represents the sacred feminine

The Virgin Mary like the Incan Pachamama is the tangible aspect of God at the top of the Catholic hierarchy in Bolivia and much of South America. She is often pictured above an upwards curved crescent moon.

energies of the body. Her watery background and robes connect her to *jing* essence. Behind her, pomegranate images upon the tapestry show their fruitful essence or seed. This is the universal symbol for the womb linked in Greek myth to the Queen of the Underworld (or Inner world), Persephone.[2] Crescent moons, sarcophagi, boats and bowls represent the feminine creative impulse in the Egyptian Mysteries.[32] The upward turned crescent moon in the card is a container for heavenly energies and is synonymous with the lower *dan tian*. We find the moon below the High Priestess collecting the heavenly rain or manna of immortality. Statues and paintings of the Virgin Mary throughout South America show her similarly situated above a crescent moon. Known for her miracles, the Mother Mary reflects the creative, manifestation of God in the physical world. Through the body we can ultimately birth the Christ-ed one within. The palm trees in the tapestry symbolize the resurrection of a savior becoming immortal.[2] In addition to the palm trees, the High Priestess shows her status as bringer of Christ consciousness by the cross symbol at the sacred heart center of the middle *dan tian*.

Circa 25,000 to 20,000 BCE, we also find the image of a full bellied Goddess figure holding an upward-turned crescent-shaped horn in one hand and pointing with the other to her lower abdomen. Painted blood red, the color of the kundalini and the

> The Venus of Laussel image carving from 25,000 – 20,000 BCE marks the entrance to a cave in Southern France. Painted red for life and blood she holds a crescent moon like container in her right hand and points to her large rounded abdomen with her left. The moon is shown to be associated with the lower dan tian in qigong theory. The carving may depict the means to spiritual rebirth through the accumulation of essence in the body and the timelessness of the mythical dimension that guides us through dreams as it did our earliest ancestors.

cinnabar elixir field, this Venus of Laussel image guards a cave entrance in France.[33] The lower abdomen as a vessel for celestial energies has archetypal significance for spiritual rebirth as far back as the Paleolithic period. Could it be that our first images of humanity show the alchemical process to spiritual rebirth? And that our ancient ancestors knew that by entering a cave they were symbolically entering the womb of the earth to create central *qi*? It would make sense as spiral pictographs have also been found marking various cave entrances around the world. These early records of spiritual ritual reflect a timeless wisdom from the collective unconscious, equivalent to the modern tarot card illustrations seen today.

The High Priestess comes in many shapes and forms in the Dreamtime, drawing upon a wealth of sacred images and symbols of past and present cultures. I have received her guidance in numerous aspects including the Sheila Na Gig image placed upon doors and archways of Catholic Churches found

> Sheela Na Gig images were fairly common above Christian church entrances in Ireland and England. Their emphasis on the vulva supports the Taoist concept of acupoint CV-1 as the doorway to our spiritual unfolding.

throughout Ireland. This goddess, with her overtly opened and emphasized vagina, also depicts the perineum floor as a gateway to the personal spiritual experience.

Chapter 11

Justice

Dream 5: I am in my bedroom in the house of my childhood. A crocodile is chasing my dog and trying to eat her. Trying to protect my dog, I shove her under my bed and away from the crocodile's jaws.

Dream 6: A man looking down from atop a wooden pole sees muddy water several feet below. Suddenly a crocodile breaks through the thick and dried layer of mud allowing the waters to clear. The man atop the pole is surprised and watches as the crocodile swims away, tail moving behind in a serpentine fashion.

Dream 7: Lucidly dreaming around dawn one morning, I see myself in a floating basket upon the banks of a river. I can feel tall reeds around the basket where I lie. A crocodile comes gently up to my basket then pushes the basket free from where it was held amongst the reeds. Guiding me through the river, the crocodile leads me towards the steps of a temple rising out of the water. The crocodile then picks up the basket with me calmly watching from within and carries me out of the river. Ascending a few steps, she places me carefully upon the ground before leaving and returning to her watery world.

Since I was a child, crocodiles have appeared as the antagonist in my dreams (though, ironically, I tried to climb into an alligator enclosure when I was about five years old). Dream 5 of this three part sequence occurred when I was a teenager. I was naturally very frightened during and following this and similar night-mares. At the time, I did not have Qigong or other tools to work through my fears and emotional obstacles. I chose to deal with emotional crisis by stuffing my emotions within myself. Not knowing how to constructively express emotional hardship, I shoved my childhood hurts and issues (like my childhood dog) into the darkness of my personal subconscious or the mythical Underworld. There they lay, metaphorically, beneath the bed where no one could see them.

Left alone, unresolved issues will eventually fester and rebel subconsciously, affecting both nighttime dreams and daily existence. The longer destructive subconscious issues are ignored, I have learned, the more challenging the dreams and experiences become in an attempt to wake the individual up to the importance of finding resolution with one's past. We release past events so they no longer hold power over or immobilize us. Freeing up and clearing our issues, we can be more authentic and natural in our expression.

As I began working with my dreams, I developed a symbolic vocabulary to understand the language of my individual dreamscape. With time, my understanding deepened and matured. I later recognized that the fearful creatures of my dreams, such as the crocodile, were in reality benevolent figures helping me get in touch with and let go of toxic emotions in my body: the storage house of my subconscious issues.

At the time of dream 6, I was an adult actively using Spiral Qigong to clear and transmute blockages in my energy system as they arose. The man on the pole shows me that I have made progress in clearing and transcending some of the emotional residue of my past. Sitting and observing from atop the pole, showing my higher level perspective, I am no longer engulfed by the fearful emotions as I was in the earlier dream experience. Rather, I am surprised at the effectiveness of the crocodile as a metal element representative to break through and clear away my old issues. The metal element in dreams is often the destructive healing power of the serpent spiral. Facilitating a spiritual breakthrough by going through the mud, I know I will have greater clarity and insight in my life as a result. The dream also signals that the crocodile's Dreamtime visits will diminish the more I actively work on my emotional clearing, as shown by the animal's swimming away into the distance. The snake-like movement of the tail reminds me that this emotional resolution came via the kundalini energies of Spiral Qigong.

At the time of dream 6, I recognized a pattern to my dreaming. Following a crocodile dream, I knew the opportunity for clearing a subconscious issue would soon arrive. The issue at hand would typically arise through a nightmare message and or as an inexplicable fog, as if there was mud covering over and plugging up my emotions around my body. If left unresolved, however, I might eventually experience an uncomfortable life lesson with someone or an unwanted event that would trigger the original subconscious perceived wounding to come to the surface. Fortunately, using Qigong Dreaming, I can now promptly release the issue with resolution experienced through greater emotional fluidity or by a subsequent positive dream, sometimes during the night only minutes or hours later. While it happens infrequently, when I now feel emotionally off balance or disconnected, I know something is ready to shift and clear from my body. It is an opportunity to use Qigong Dreaming for self healing. Like a snake, I am getting ready to shed my old skin and be symbolically reborn. Behaviorally, snakes also experience irritability and an opaque haziness over their eyes prior to molting. In releasing their old skin, snakes clear scars and mites from their bodies and literally emerge stronger, larger and healthier.

In dream 7, the crocodile is now clearly an ally and helper. The prior fearfulness caused by this messenger was clearly only an illusion (keep this in mind with real people who trigger your stuff). Having developed my emotional intelligence, I have an easier time expressing uncomfortable thoughts and feelings so they don't become lodged within my body in the first place. Moving more fluidly through the water rather than stuck amongst the reeds, I act more spontaneously and have greater peace in my life. The spiritual gifts of my kundalini awakening are now surfacing consciously to mind as shown by the crocodile moving me up the steps of a temple. The crocodile is clearly another aspect of the High Priestess offering her gifts of transformative healing. I note the similarity of dream 7 to Moses' floating in a basket. Moses may have also been spiritually initiated into new levels of awareness by feminine intuition and sacred dreaming. Similarities between the Bible and dreams reaffirm to me that the two are derived from Source and can be interpreted symbolically.

The Justice card is similar to the Judgment of the Dead found in the Egyptian *Book of the Dead*. This book details how at death, the heart soul (*ab*) of the deceased is placed within one of the scale pans and weighed against the feather of Maat, the goddess of truth and justice, in the other pan.[2] If the soul of the dead was heavier than Spirit, it was given to a fearsome crocodile-like creature to be swallowed and consumed. If, however, the heart was as light or pure as the feather, the individual could become immortal like the resurrected god Osiris and ascend to heaven. Maat provides divine insight into the purity of the heart and the crocodile is a symbol for the transformative quality of the alchemical process. The man-god Osiris who lived within a perfect body resided over the ceremonial weighing. He gave eternal life to the souls of humankind who had transformed their bodies and purified their hearts, making them incorruptible.[34]

Each time we work out an aspect of our destructive subconscious, we lighten our soul, particularly the *yin* soul of the metal element in Chinese Medicine theory. Clearing the seven related emotions (fear, fright, anger, overexcitement, worry, sadness and grief) we lighten and harmonize with Spirit. According to myth, if we do not resolve our stuff, we may be due for another cycle on the karmic wheel of fortune as we take our emotional baggage with us when we die. Liberation found in awakening the

> The crocodile faced Egyptian god Sobek at Kom Ombo Temple was said to teach the (alchemical) art of gold making to the ancient Egyptians. There is a line dividing the temple of Kom Ombo between the crocodile god Sobek and the hawk faced god Haroeris. The eyes and ears show that the gods watch and listen to ensure equal homage to the physical and spiritual aspects of ourselves. Image shown in Chapter 22.

consciousness of the body provides promise of eternal life and ascension upon death.

While traveling in Egypt with Andrea Mikana-Pinkham of Sacred Sites Journeys in November 2007, I enjoyed exploring the Temple at Kom Ombo. Half of this temple is dedicated to the crocodile god Sobek while the other half is dedicated to the sun god Haroeris. As I was touring the temple, the ancient Egyptian belief in the importance of equally honoring the physical (crocodile god) and spiritual (sun god) was apparent. There was even a centerline demarcation within the temple showing that the gods and goddesses were watching and listening to ensure that proper balance was maintained. As legend goes, the crocodile god Sobek taught the people how to grow gold and enjoy physical abundance while the sun god Haroeris educated the people on how to grow food and cultivate their spiritual nature. The refinement of the physical into gold and the development of spiritual virtues resemble quite closely the inner alchemy of the Chinese Taoists.

In ancient Egypt, the purification of the *ka* body is equivalent to the Chinese *po* soul. As there were Chinese medical procedures such as cupping and needles (acupuncture needles perhaps) upon the opposing walls of the temple and many sculpted deities with Asian characteristics, there appear to be many cross cultural similarities likely from the sharing of ideas.

The Temple of Kom Ombo is known archeologically as a place

> Egyptian Mystery initiates overcame their fear of death swimming in crocodile infested underground tunnels at Kom Ombo. In dreams we also face and overcome our fears.

where initiates swam in crocodile inhabited waters to face and overcome their fears. Through rituals, initiates swam through darkened underground tunnels, symbolic gateways to the *xuan* or Collective Unconscious. Reemerging several meters later above ground and into the light, they experienced a sort of spiritual renewal. Maybe the images of women giving birth within the temple of Kom Ombo also depict the use of internal cultivation techniques to rebirth. They are, after all, shown sitting in a position that opens CV-1 in an initiatory temple.

The Sword of Justice highlights the importance of the element metal. Like the large intestine of the body, it has the function of separating the clear from the turbid. Helping us let go of what is no longer needed, what we release becomes fertilizer for the earth.[12] Shown in hexagram 23 of the I Ching as 'splitting apart', the metal element represents the destructive and reconstructive nature of the inner alchemical works. By releasing the old, there is space for rebirth and renewal of the higher self. Dream images of rocks, graves, toilets, sinks, shower drains, trash dumpsters, minefields, predatory animals, teeth, metal weapons, knives, mountainous trolls and other metal images may highlight the need to release emotional issues from the psyche.

Many sacred sites around the world are natural or architectural works of the metal element. Mountains, caves, megalithic structures, pyramids, obelisks, temples and cathedrals have all been spiritual places of worship throughout the ages. The geologic anomalies and unusual magnetic or radiation fluctuation have been recorded at many sacred sites around the world.[35] Often marked in sacred geometric patterns and symbols, some like the Temple of Delphi in Greece were associated with large snakes and used for oracular guidance. Through ecstatic trance the oracles could communicate and honor the gods.[35] I have experienced heightened intuitive awareness and dreaming at the pyramids and temples of Egypt, at the aboriginal heart of Australia called Uluru and at Mt Shasta, a holy site to Native Californians. This is the dreaming or intuitive aspect of the metal element. Our awareness of their influence on dreaming heightens as we clear the subtle energies flowing through our bodies.

In Egypt, the red granite from the city of Aswan was cut to build the sarcophagus in the king's chamber of the Great Pyramid and other holy of holies throughout the country. People also traveled long distances to bring specific stones to Stonehenge in England and hard to reach mountain-topped temples in Peru. Granite, found at many sacred sites, is known to release higher levels of gamma radiation. Research into the effects of different stones at ancient sites upon the brain and body would offer interesting insight into the effects of metals and geologic factors upon nonlinear thinking and intuition. It might also help clarify the uses of these sacred sites.

Chapter 12

The Moon

This Peruvian Ouroborus shows the moon and snake as equivalent symbols of death and resurrection revolving counterclockwise around the eternal symbol of the sun.

Joseph Campbell compared the light of the moon to the immortal and eternal light within the body.[28] Lao Tzu would likely agree as the freeing of body consciousness is the way back to the eternal light of the Tao. Through Qigong we give ourselves an internal energetic shower. It is how we purify and clean the densities that slow down the natural flow of life force energy. And when we allow time in our lives for the consciousness within to express itself spontaneously we, likewise, strengthen the infinite aspect of our original nature. Energy cannot be created nor destroyed. When we raise the vibration of our physical body through internal cultivation techniques we become light like in what the Taoists call the immortal body and Albert Einstein scientifically expressed as $E=mc^2$. Being aware of ourselves as pure energy we consciously come to know the radiance of God that flows within.

In Chinese Medicine the moon is the celestial treasure of the sky just as the *jing* essence is the internal treasure of the physical body. Its influence affects the tides of the ocean as well as the waters within us. Astrologically, the moon represents those aspects of the self that are hidden or below consciousness. It has the ability to pull out the shadowy parts of our nature that cover up the light within. Our subconscious energies are the things we decide are unacceptable within our cultural, spiritual and family upbringing. Growing up, we repress certain impulses as we learn from experience what appropriate behavior and values 'should' be. This is represented by the domestic dog in the Moon card. The subconscious issues that we fear become locked away below the threshold of awareness. They are shown as the wild dog in the Moon card and may present themselves as dis-ease in our physical lives. Denied expression, they become increasingly chaotic desperately seeking to get our attention through nightmares and unsavory life experiences so they can become acknowledged and freed. The things in the night may appear scary at times unless we have good tools like Qigong to face and resolve our self-created demons. The blue lobster in the Moon card is shown rising out of the waters. Coming out onto the land, this symbol reflects our biological as well as psychological evolution. By bringing the subconscious (underwater) into conscious awareness (onto dry land) we benefit by embracing more of our innate creative gifts. The Moon reflects the light that illuminates the path to authentic living for each of us. It shows the way to find inner peace and joy in our lives. Our greatest challenges are but opportunities to grow beyond our limitations and exceed our standards of ourselves.

Many Greek goddesses such as Artemis are depicted with snakes to symbolize healing and initiation.

Dream 8: I am visiting a local wildlife area where my family and I often enjoy walking and biking. Walking alone towards the west I approach the local pond. Looking down within the waters, I see a beautiful blue fairy with wings like a butterfly and a feminine face flying slowly and gracefully underneath the surface. I am overjoyed to be seeing such magical beauty and quickly pull out my camera to take a picture. I think to myself, as I watch the fairy's movements through the lens of the camera, how wonderful it would be to share this experience with others.

The ancient Greek goddess Hekate represents the dark aspect of the moon. She is an archetypal energy helping people face and overcome their fears and illusions through destruction of the ego.

I had dream 8 the night after a five elements acupuncture appointment while I was studying Oriental Medicine. The treatment session that day had focused on awakening the *yang* Spirit (*shen*) and *yin* Spirit (*ling*) of the heart. Kidney 23, Kidney 24, and Kidney 25 are acupuncture points located on either side of the chest on the watery Kidney channel. They are also external points related to the Central Channel. Often treated together, they help maintain the proper alchemical balance between the fire and water elements of the heart.[12] Kidney 23 is known as Spirit Seal and provides a sense of purpose and spiritual identity. Kidney 24 is called Spirit Burial Ground and brings nourishing water to rejuvenate the heart. It helps the client return to Source and experience him or herself as a potent and effective force in the world. Kidney 25 is Spirit Storehouse. Stimulation of this point helps the Spirit of the heart maintain authority in the body's kingdom.[12]

Aphrodite the Greek Goddess of Love was believed to rise from the sea at her birth. Symbolically good things come into manifestation when destructive subconscious influences are faced and resolved.

Many people experience a spiritual awakening or initiation around midlife. Having grown outwardly through cultural and academic influences in the first half of life, as Carl Jung explains, the individual psyche, yearning for balance and authentic expression, will turn inward to explore the true self in the second half of life. Those not recognizing the deeper yearnings of the soul or misunderstanding the language of their dreams might feel depressed, angry, or dissatisfied with life during this time, not understanding why or what to do. This is what we call a midlife crisis. Somewhere the individual has gotten off track. The higher self is trying to rectify the disequilibrium between internal and external realities. As energies of the soul become voiced and liberated, the Dreamtime scenery reflects this. Dream guidance comes to show us our god-given gifts.

Dream 8 shows me that my *shen ling* energies are beginning to wake up. This is symbolized by the underwater movement of the feminine fairy and magical quality of the dream. The dream message rings true. Showing people how to work with their dreams and connect with themselves through Qigong Dreaming brings me great reward. Yet viewing myself as a teacher is something I strongly denied in myself a decade earlier. I know now that I find great joy and fulfillment writing this book, for example. When I feel internally driven to express myself through writing, the myriad of other things I 'should' be doing fall to the wayside. For though I enjoy helping people with various ailments in my work as an acupuncturist, I know that

Shakespeare's words in *Hamlet*, 'This above all: to thine own self be true' is the basis of true healing. Speaking from experience, I encourage everyone to dig through their own Spiritual Burial Ground to uncover the energies and talents that bring joy to their heart.

Looking through the camera lens in the above dream, I see the black Ouroborus once more on the periphery. Rediscovering my intuition and the magical quality of life, symbolized by the fairy in my dream, I can find our way home.

My first experience with the blue fairy occurred the summer between high school and the beginning of college, when my mom's roommate took me to a chakra meditation class. The topic of the evening was the sixth chakra, the Hindu energy wheel relating to sight and spiritual vision in the forehead. I didn't know what a chakra was or what we were doing. I remember liking the rocks called crystals the instructor had brought and that we closed our eyes and 'meditated', focusing on our breathing for a little while. I probably wouldn't even remember the experience except that night while getting ready for bed, I saw an etheric blue fairy appear and float across my room. Though she was small, I saw the varied blue hues of her dress and facial features quite clearly. Once again, my personal experience authenticated and adjusted my concept of reality.

> *Dream 9: I am underwater in a large pool with my daughter. Other people I don't recognize are in the pool as well. I see a large orca whale circling around amongst us. As the orca is moving close to my teenage daughter, I step in front of the whale to protect her. Seeing me, the whale begins checking me out with its tongue. It tries to put its mouth around me to taste or sense me. Wanting to maintain some control and my life, I back up against the side of the pool. I find that bracing against the wall I can stretch my body upwards and maneuver above the whale's mouth. Moving more effectively in this watery environment, I feel confident and safe.*

I had this dream prior to taking some Watsu training from a nearby friend. Watsu is Shiatsu bodywork in the medium of water. In both cases pressure instead of needles is used to open the energy channels and acupoints of the body. I looked at the training as an opportunity to do spontaneous Qigong in a liquid medium, something that happens quite naturally for me. In a past Watsu session, I had moved wildly about though not very efficiently for over ninety minutes. By the end of my session I was physically and emotionally depleted. Though it had been extremely beneficial in clearing my body and voice (some good screaming and crying resulted) it took too much time and energy. I also needed an extra hour following the session to recover so I was fit to drive home. In dream 9, I am given the guidance to use my Central Channel to ground the energies as they move through me. In so doing I can more easily and efficiently clear my inner child issues as represented by my daughter in the dream. I recognized the meaning of the dream when in the pool later that day during a practice session I began once again flailing about. Using my intention to ground my Central Channel into the earth, I had an anchor point for my muscles to contract around facilitating the spontaneous releases. What a difference! I could clear my energy system quickly and easily walk out of the pool. With additional practice also came greater proficiency with Qigong until movements became almost completely unnecessary in the clearing work. Then using the power of the mind, I learned that Qigong Dreaming could shift discordant energies in seconds. (More details on mind over matter healing appears in Section B – The Virtues of *Yang*.)

Chapter 13

The Devil

The first of the seven major Tantric etheric energy centers, called chakras, is often located between the sexual organs and the anus. This is the root base of the body called the *Muladhara*. The following picture of the root chakra shows a red downward pointing triangle or yoni, in the center of the image.[28] This symbol of the womb is also the regenerative organ of the Great Mother explains Joseph Campbell. Here at the root chakra we experience the time - space aspect of the cosmos. However, within the yoni is the male sexual organ counterpart, the lingam encircled by a serpent. According to Campbell this lingam represents the Hindu god Shiva and the energy of the transcendental that entering the womb unites male and female opposites to return to oneness consciousness.[28] This is the foundation of body consciousness where feminine and masculine fuse together to generate the upward ascension energies of the kundalini along the *Sushumna* channel, which is comparable to the Governing Vessel of the spine. Represented by the Sanskrit letter *lam* the root chakra is also the manifestation power of the universe. The elephant's trunk is shaped like a snake. Pointing downward it may reflect the descent of creative energies along the Conception Vessel.

> The root chakra shows the kundalini serpent encircling a stone lingam, comparable to the rise of serpent power within the popular Hindu deity Shiva. Working with the transcendental aspect of the spiral symbol is a means to break free of ego trappings and the symbolic chains that bind us.

In certain myths, the elephant could originally fly but is currently earthbound and holding up the universe.[28] Notice that the elephant within the root chakra is bound around the neck by a thin black necklace or cord. Hanging from the cord is a small bell, a musical instrument for making sound vibration. It is our job to free up the dormant life force energies that we keep bound and repressed. The elephant is all white as a representation of the metal element. Liberating the seven emotions of the *yin* soul, one liberates the authentic self for greater health and zest for life. The bell around the neck is a clue that perhaps freedom occurs via the fifth chakra. Called *Visuddha,* it means pure. Located behind the throat the fifth chakra controls the principle of sound in the body and the universe.[36]

The fifth chakra clears and opens the physical being to the experience of transcendence.[28] Here again we find the white elephant, who also happens to be associated with the moon. No longer bound around the neck in fifth chakra images, he has found freedom of expression from hidden tendencies. The multiple trunks cascade freely up and down now, showing the free flow of energy within the Central Channel and along the microcosmic orbit.

The presiding deity of the fifth chakra is androgynous, showing balance of *yin* and *yang* principles. The right half in white is the transcendental aspect of Shiva and the left half in gold is his goddess consort Shakti.[36] The deity may represent the realized immortal golden body united with universal consciousness.

Dream 10: I see the image of a black dog with a choke collar around his neck running playfully towards the left side of my field of vision. Suddenly a man's hand coming from the right violently yanks the leash, pulling the dog cruelly backwards.

Dream 11: I see an image of myself. There is a large boa constrictor wrapped around my neck choking me.

Dream 12: I am painting a picture of myself with watercolors. Directing the paintbrush, I try to paint my throat. While the other parts of the picture pick up different color, my neck remains colorless.

Dream 13: I am in the Coast Guard and going in for a checkup. I am told I have a lump on the left hand of my thyroid. Further checkups reveal that I have a small benign tumor there.

Soon after returning from the extraordinary vision described in dream 1, I had a series of dreams about my throat including dreams 10, 11 and 12. My dreams were informing me that I had been cutting off my own self expression. In dream 10, I was both the dog trying to run free and the hand that controlled the animal's movements. The dog is black and represents something I was not aware of consciously. The dream signals that something is wrong and my psyche is trying to correct the imbalance and move to the left, for greater creative intuitive thinking. However, my right, linear structured thinking is dominating the situation and my life. It hinders the natural and free movements of the dog or my animal instincts. I am off kilter, and all four dreams alert me that a change is needed. I thought at the time that dreams 11 and 12 were simply repeating the same message of dream 10: that I had a bogged down fifth chakra from stuffing my emotional and creative expression for years. However, in hindsight, I recognized they were also providing a clue to help me remove the self imposed chains around my own neck. Dream 11 showed the power of the spiraling central *qi* as a snake to transmute the inner poisons of my fifth chakra. Dream 12 depicted that through creative movement of the paintbrush, symbolizing my Qigong work with the Central Channel, that visual images or dreams would be produced. The throat being devoid of color represented the void of the Tao expressed through the voice. I would learn about the potency of sound and voice healing several years later.

Dream 13 was a real event that happened a year following the other dreams. I include it to demonstrate the weaving of the Dreamtime in waking life. We can examine all events for symbolic or divinatory meaning as we do our nighttime dreams. Dream 13 was a continuation of prior dreams whereby the unresolved issues moved into physical form. Though I was getting back on track pursuing an exciting and more authentic new career in Oriental Medicine, I still had garbage in the energetic plumbing, so to speak, that needed to be cleared. My subconscious emotional baggage had transitioned into physical symptoms, becoming more insistent to get my attention and be healed. How appropriate that the tumor was found on the left side of my throat, the same side seeking expression (and restrained) by the dog figure in dream 10.

The following Hindu myth describes the creation of the nectar of immortality and how Shiva, the wild god of power and ecstasy, acquired his blue throat.

Long, long ago, the eternal antagonists, demons and gods, were fighting. The guru of the demons was awakening all the fallen demons and titans and bringing them back to life. The gods were soon outnumbered and scared for their lives. They decided they needed the ambrosia of immortality called *amrita* from the depths of the ocean of milk to save them.[10] The gods did not have sufficient power to churn the seas alone and enlisted the help of their adversaries, the demons. Using the world mountain as the churning stick, Ananta, the endless world serpent, wrapped his body around the rope. With the gods holding the head and the demons holding the tail of this Lord of the Underworld, they worked together to churn the waters by pulling back and forth in a type of tug of war.[10]

One of the first things that bubbled up out of the waters was the poison of the world. It threatened all of creation. The terrified gods quickly went to find the god Shiva, who was meditating upon his sacred mountain. Shiva calmly opened his eyes and drank the poison in one big gulp. His goddess consort, Parvati,

> The rise of kundalini helps remove destructive tendencies blocking healthy expression and is represented by the snake wrapped around the neck of Shiva, the Hindu god of destruction.

was there too and out of concern, she clasped her hands about Shiva's neck closing it shut.[10] Stuck in his neck, the poisons transformed Shiva's throat to an aquamarine blue, the color associated with the fifth chakra. The gods and demons then proceeded with their churning and out came a number of wondrous things including the tree of paradise, the moon, the goddess of love, beauty and prosperity and the physician of the gods coveting the cup of ambrosia.[10] Within his hands he held the means to ageless immortality.

The union of yin and yang opposites is symbolized in the above myth by the demons and gods. Only by uniting together through the churning of the Central Channel can heat be generated to bring subconscious issues out of the hidden waters and into consciousness. The unified central *qi* helps transmute the toxins of the self and the world. Through Spiral Qigong our destructive tendencies can be digested and transformed through spontaneous verbal expression at the throat. Parvati as a Hindu goddess personifies the kundalini clearing of the fifth chakra. Energy healing has moved to the upper part of the body. Clearing out the throat there is greater access to powerful spiritual energies from above. Allowing spontaneous sounds to be verbalized through Spiral Qigong is a great purifying technique. The story shows that following the alchemical cleansing process many rewards follow including intuitive gifts (moon), love, youthfulness and abundance (goddess), good health (physician), spiritual rebirth in heaven (tree of paradise), and everlasting life through the immortal golden body (the cup or grail of ambrosia).

Dream 14: I see the profile of my head. There is a black cord about my neck. As I watch, the cord slowly disappears and is replaced by a loose gold necklace with an infinity pendant made of diamonds.

Sacred dreaming will often incorporate aspects of spiritual myth in addition to sacred symbols to convey the appropriate meaning. All spiritual wisdom comes from the collective unconscious of the Dreamtime. In dream 14, my psyche is showing that I have removed the cord of bondage around my neck having purified the fifth chakra. Using spontaneous vocalizations that day in Qigong class, I removed emotional blockages and transmuted disharmonious energies. Having further cleared my Central Channel, my fifth chakra is open to channel the omnipotence of the infinite Tao. The deity of the fifth chakra is androgynous, as discussed previously in this chapter. The white color of the god and the gold color of the goddess united were also depicted in dream 14 to show the newfound health of my throat chakra following Spiral Qigong practice.

Dream 15: I am dancing playfully and seductively up close with the actor Matthew McConaughey and having a great time.

The male and female characters of the Devil card bring to mind the concept of shame and sexuality associated with the fall of Adam and Eve. Many friends, family and students I know have shared feeling a sense of guilt regarding sexually explicit dreams. I remind them that the dream world works in the language of the symbolic and typically the dreams are not to be interpreted literally. Intimate dreams reflect the yearning for communion with creative and spiritual energies we inhibit within ourselves. The energies are often personified in dreams with certain individuals we view as possessing the traits we admire, having dissociated from owning them ourselves. The higher self, trying to reintegrate all mentally separated aspects, will sometimes use sexual connotations to represent reunion. I thought Matthew McConaughey was charismatic and charming and admired him for his former wild bongo playing pursuits. The fact that he didn't seem to care about public opinion seemed most appealing. While happily monogamous in my married life, there was, however, an internal drive to likewise let go and be spontaneous in my body's actions that my dream with Matthew reflected. Dreams help us identify those energies seeking reconciliation. Spiral Qigong can then help remove the self limiting psychological blocks that bind and restrict us. As the above dream points out, being one's true self includes physical freedom of expression.

Dr. Christiane Northrup writes in *Mother Daughter Wisdom* that authentic sexuality is linked to self worth and how we value ourselves and our bodies. Dr. Mona Lisa Shultz connects sexuality to different parts of the brain and describes how sexual energy is a biological force affecting creativity, sharing and self expression.[37] Self expression through movement liberates our instincts and the sense of joy we receive from being consciousness incarnate in physical form. Increasing inner awareness, we connect with the wisdom of our bodies and unlock the spiritual dimension to our sensuous nature that we had previously been unconscious of. Intimate postures of male and female deities are prevalent as statues in India. Honoring the lingam and yoni, people consecrate their bodies to a transcendental God. In China, overt sexuality in art reflects the physical union of *yin* and *yang* as a means to return to primordial oneness consciousness. We can let go of our thinking mind when we can physically and emotionally connect with someone outside ourselves that we love. Ecstatic orgasm will also naturally contract CV-1 and can with intention be a Qigong Dreaming technique, channeling vital energy to a situation in need of healing. Sending positive intentions into the world with the electromagnetic impulse generated can be a powerful creative act.

As Dr. Linda Savage, author of *Reclaiming Goddess Sexuality,* explains that sexual energy is the foundation to our connection with all of life.[37] I have found this to be true and encourage the spiritual seeker to purify concepts of body image and sexuality as it is an important part of the spiritual journey. I can attest that intimacy with my husband has reached new levels of bliss and satisfaction beyond anything I had experienced. While not the primary purpose for my doing Spiral Qigong, letting go of being in control and rigid cultural belief systems has led to greater joy and fulfillment with what can be a very sacred and joyful union.

The male and female figures in the Devil card have the option to remove the chains around their necks and be free and liberated. They will likely have to discard negative cultural and religious stereotypes about their bodies, about their sexuality and about their intuitive natures as well as limiting dualistic concepts of good and evil. Episcopal Priest Morton Kelsey writes about the sacredness of sexuality teaching that through desire we recognize longing for union with that which is hidden within ourselves, and through us with God.[37] It is time that we liberate the archetype of Eve, Mary Magdalene and the serpent within ourselves. Regardless of gender we have been stereotyped with psychological energies degraded by dominant peer, family and religious influences for a long time. Further suppression of healthy sexuality and intuition within individuals and a culture is harmful. By allowing suppressed instincts to rise out of the dark corners of the subconscious, the couple in the Devil card can reunite back into oneness consciousness. Purging the inhibitions of the soul we can each move beyond limiting labels of good versus evil for greater joy and peace of mind.

Dream 16: Jesus appears and tells me the serpent is an aspect of himself.

Dream 16 came at a time when I was clearing some limiting religious ideas held below the threshold of my conscious mind about the devil figure of Christianity. I do not believe in the Devil and view sin as perceived separation from God. However, I was having a fair number of snake and dragon dreams at the time, and there was a little concern in the back of my mind that perhaps this was not 'good'. I share this dream experience as others embarking on a spiritual quest will likely encounter their own devilish figures or issues in the dreamscape and projected life experience encounters. I recommend looking beyond the illusion of duality. Rather than blaming the dream messenger try looking within to see what the dream or person reflects about your inner world. Isn't the Devil symbol, with his hoofed feet and hairy legs, a scapegoat figure after all? Be thankful for the opportunity to be more self aware and look to release the lower frequency issue that attracted the experience to you in the first

The serpent haired Medusa is commonly found upon ancient sarcophagi in Greece and Turkey as a symbol of protection to ward off looters and unsavory influences. One of Medusa's blue eyes later became the protective evil eye to many Muslims and Christians.

place via the microcosm – macrocosm interrelationship. It is only by looking inward to resolve the issue that we allow our karma to come to the surface. We then have the option to clear what it reflects about ourselves and our fears.

Chapter 14

Death

Dream 17: Looking down from my balcony, I see my cat with a bird on his shoulder in the backyard. They are secretly talking together unaware that I can see them. I recognize they are friends taking a break from the play they are performing in as actors. Soon break-time ends and they start getting ready to resume their roles.

Dealing with death has not been an easy thing for me. Having grown up in the suburbs of California, I did not comprehend the naturalness of death as an integral part of life as many people growing up on farms do. Distraught when my cat Buddy, whom we affectionately called Death, brought home his little feathered gifts, the above dream came to teach me an important lesson. Death and suffering experienced through the five senses is what the Hindus call *maya* or the veil of illusion. Recognizing our chosen parts in this collective performance, we have the opportunity to grow and evolve. Through awareness of the infinite intelligence of the Tao, we begin to remove the illusory veil and come to know there is more to this existence than meets the eye. Resolving our relationship with death, one of our greatest fears and spiritual blocks, we flow and synchronize more fluidly through the cycle of nature for greater participation in life. Though I did not appreciate my cat's predatory nature, he provided an opportunity for me to overcome my resistance and mature.

Dream 18: I had the following lucid dream while practicing a still form of meditation during a weekend retreat. Sitting cross-legged on the floor with eyes closed I focus on my breathing. About half an hour later the image of a raven appears in my mind. I ask 'Who are you?' After a moment's pause, I hear back, 'I am Raven.' I proceed to ask, 'Who am I?' The response heard audibly in my head is 'Impermanence.'

The word 'alchemy' is derived from the word *al kimia* and is translated by some authorities as 'the art of the black land'. The ancient people of Egypt referred to their land as KMT or Khemit meaning 'the Black Land'.[38] This link between what we now call Egypt and alchemy also highlights the first process of alchemy called *Nigredo* or the black stage. This is the first step of the Lesser Work, whereby matter is transformed from a chaotic state to a higher level of organization. The black stage is symbolized in alchemical art and text by the *caput mortuum* or death's head.[3] The black armored skeleton figure on horseback in the 13th tarot card represents this first step in the gold or god making process. The raven, as seen in dream 18, is another traditional symbol for *Nigredo,* whereby the raw and destructive aspects of matter go through a spiritual and metaphysical metamorphosis[3].

The Aztec Calendar from the Great Temple of Mexico depicts a central skull representing the eternal devouring void in the center of an ouroborus. Mayan calendars mark the cycles of time.

The second phase of the Lesser Work is called *Albedo.* This is the whitening or cleansing of matter that supersedes death.[3] White is the color of the metal element in Chinese Medicine and the feminine *yin* body soul. This whitening corresponds to the purification of the *po* soul. *Albedo* is often represented in alchemical illustrations by the old king drowning in water to allow the young prince to emerge. So it is that in the Death card, we see the dead king lying adjacent to a pool of water. The young child in blue represents the newly emerging spiritual consciousness achieved through the sacrifice of the figuratively old and outdated parts of ourselves.

The horse represents the union of the world of the immanent with the state of the transcendent. Though he carries death upon his back, the horse's eyes are spiritual windows reflecting the eternal light of the sun. Having let go or deathed impurities and restrictions around his fifth throat chakra (skull and crossbones around the neck), the horse represents impermanence.

Staying in the present is a constant process of releasing (deathing) the past. Remaining mentally fluid also means being undeterred by worries and concerns about the future. Maintaining awareness beyond the concepts of time one can experience the freedom and peace from going with the flow. Surrendering up the ego's mental control one begins to see and experience (like the horse in this card) the hidden truth of an eternal reality.

Dream 19: I am back in Egypt and given a folder. Written on the cover is a note from Abd'El Hakim Awyan, an indigenous Khemitian Wisdom Keeper and one of my teachers during my travels through Egypt. His writings tell me my gift is earth healing. I look in another room and see Hakim walk from my right to my left, from the east to the west. I think how fortunate I am to see him again as he has recently transitioned from physical life. I am later up among the stars with Hakim. I see a part of myself as the priest officiating at Hakim's marriage-like ceremony of union with God.

Dream 19 illuminated my understanding of death. I felt very fortunate to witness the mystical union of soul and Spirit of this great traditional teacher of pre-dynastic Egyptian wisdom following his transition a week earlier. In the dream I play the role of the golden-clad priest of the Death card, who is guiding the ceremony. In this card, the priest addresses the individual on horseback in a spiritual ritual similar to marriage. From this perspective the individual on horseback in the Death card has transitioned and is reuniting with God, the transcendental oneness that has no image. So it was also in my dream that I only saw Hakim at the spiritual union and the final alchemical stage of *Rubedo*.

The horse and rider are of gigantic stature on the card making the priest appear insignificant by comparison. To me, this is also a warning not to relinquish inner power and spiritual connection to external religious figureheads or teachers. They may facilitate but it is the responsibility of each individual to access their own inner teacher and learn firsthand through personal experience. Cultivating our intuitive skills we connect with the infinite intelligence of the universe directly. As Lao Tzu explains we can access the deepest secrets of the universe without even leaving our home.

A five petal flower (like that on the Death card) decorates the remains of a column at the Temple of Apollo at Pamukkale, Turkey. The vaporous steam rising from subterranean rivers induced visionary trances for the oracles at this site. The Temple of Delphi in Greece was the most famous oracle site of western civilization. Here the oracles were known to receive wisdom from a subterranean snake called Python.

The Death card reaffirms divine feminine intuition and the awareness of the dream state. The rider carries the five-petaled flower, a symbol of the five elements of nature. Being white in color it also represents the feminine qualities of introspection. The rider's downward directed red plume shows Death's allegiance to mother earth. Through nature and our physical bodies we come to learn about spiritual rebirth.

It is the youthful child who with unfettered innocence calmly

Skeletal remains were buried in large red vases in the Bronze Age in Turkey. This tomb was symbolic of the womb of the Great Goddess and thought to help initiate spiritual rebirth

faces death in this card. The boy holds the golden mean spiral, also known as phi, and the divine proportion. The phi ratio is the evolutionary aspect of the central *qi* behind all of nature. Phi also symbolizes spiritualized matter leading to the doorway to love in the heart.[31] The child thus holds the key to the mysteries of the universe within his hands.

The youth also holds the arm of the young maiden behind him. She is the personified dreaming aspect of the boy who happily journeys to the collective unconscious. In the dream state she learns the wisdom of the ages, that death and life are two sides of the same coin. Having entered the gateway to the *xuan*, depicted by the boat floating midstream between *yin* (lush) and *yang* (dry) lands, her serenity reflects arcane knowledge of what alchemists describe as 'the mightiest secret that a man [or woman] can possess'.

Dream 20: I am on my back in the middle of a square bed that is low to the floor in an unfamiliar room. Looking about me, I see that I am under blankets and there are a total of four candles around me (at my feet, head and on either side of me). My Watsu instructor is standing

There is a spiral scroll held by an angel above Jesus' head on a fresco of Judgment Day at the Chora Church in Istanbul, Turkey representing Paradise. Like the Chinese concept of central qi this spiral shows the sun and moon depicted within the spiral and the unity of opposites leading to transcendence.

next to me beside a large mirror. She tells me, 'You need to speak to the mirror.' After a momentary silence, my instructor responds, 'The mirror says it is time and you are ready.' I suddenly remember my kids and looking at my watch realize I am late picking them up from school. I promptly excuse myself from the ceremony and get off the bed. Nearby, I see my mom. She tells me everything is all right. I look once more at my watch and realize with relief that I have an extra hour. I have lots of time and need not have worried about my children.

The Virgin Mary appeared in a dream to Tito Yupanqui in 1576 and led to the construction of a church in her honor. The Virgen de Copacabana Church is the most important church in Bolivia. People from all around South America make a pilgrimage to this cathedral to receive her blessings.

Initiations are powerful rituals helping facilitate transitions in our lives. We are each in transition in some way as our time here on Earth is subject to perpetual change. Whether with family, work, friendships, or interests, something in our lives is cycling through one of four primary phases. We are in this sense impermanent with a part of ourselves; birthing, developing, maturing, or releasing as we physically, emotionally and spiritually adapt to our changing environment.

Indigenous, pagan, mystery traditions and orthodox religions validate and celebrate different rites of passage. It is through our second birth of spiritual renewal that we symbolically break from the physical mother, recognizing and honoring our relationship with unlimited Source. Spiritual rebirth may be instantaneous but most often it is a journey or process.

Regardless, it involves letting go of limiting thoughts, material attachments and fears, especially concerning mortality. This is why rituals of symbolic death have been prevalent in all cultures around the world for ages. Some rituals that I have benefited from include college graduation, spring cleaning, giving away of old clothing, sweat lodges, spiritual pilgrimages, labyrinth walking and going to church in honor of religious holidays. Any action with proper intention can be a symbolic ritual and facilitate transitions to a new phase of development. Like the snake shedding its skin, we let go of those things and beliefs that restrict our free movement in life. Being reborn, we emerge from our symbolic chrysalis like the butterfly, transformed and angelic with wings.

My Watsu instructor was the first person to confirm that I was undergoing what she termed a kundalini awakening. No wonder she appears as a mentor figure in dream 20. She, like any good teacher, guides the initiate to speak directly with Spirit. This mirror of my dream, like the one in the Snow White fable, can only tell the truth. It is, therefore, a symbol of the reflection of the infinite intelligence of the Tao. Source has told me that I am ready; however, my personality has some concerns that my budding spirituality will negatively impact my being there for my children in the temporal existence of normal life; thus, my concern for being late picking them up. Fortunately, my mother as the *yin* or intuitive aspect of Spirit reassures me that my concerns are illusory and I have nothing to fear.

Following dream 20, I made lunch plans with my Watsu instructor. We mutually shared some of our kundalini experiences. It was extremely helpful and validating to talk with someone who had had similar experiences with the sacred serpent power. I walked out of the café afterwards with renewed confidence, strength and joy in who I was. I was comfortable in my own skin and with my own unique path. I fell asleep that night seeing the etheric presence of my instructor kneeling next to me in support and friendship. I awoke later that night feeling the crown of my head wide open and seeing different dimensions of the Dreamtime. Accepting myself on a deeper level spurred a major leap in my spiritual growth. I saw once more as I went back to sleep the ceremonial candles from dream 20. I watched the wind blow them out knowing the initiation begun earlier in the dream state was now complete.

After dream 20, I wondered if I was being directed to find a teacher or program of study. I looked around and even interviewed different groups but nothing felt right. Rather than looking outside for instruction, however, I came to realize that what I needed was accessible through Qigong and dreaming. I was to communicate directly with God as explained in the dialogue with the mirror in the dream. As Lao Tzu taught, all the answers can be found within. Initiation is first and foremost an internal process originating from God.

Chapter 15

Judgment

Dream 21: In group meditation I see an upright rectangular sarcophagus of gray stone. The door opens and a mummy figure wrapped up in white gauze emerges very much alive. As he stands there the white wrappings fade away until nothing remains. The dream imagery transforms and I see deep space. Among the stars are brilliant red and blue hues in the dark sky.

This is just one of the many death-to-spiritual rebirth dreams I experienced during the early part of my alchemical kundalini awakening. Death is merely a transition from physical form to more subtle states of existence. Transcending the death - rebirth cycle completely, we can return to the heavenly stars, the highest aim of the ancients. Spiritual death dream experiences such as this help us overcome the fears of our own mortality and spiritually mature. Rather than representing impending physical death, however, as many dreamers worry, the symbolic meaning reflects psychological work and the positive releasing of old ways of thinking and behaving. Through alchemical cleansing, the soul regenerates and rejuvenates naturally.

Dream 21 reminded me of the Judgment card and reaffirmed the dream-tarot-alchemy connection. The mummy shows that I am beginning to awaken the dead aspects within myself. The disappearance of white colored gauze shows a couple things. Alchemy is the dissolution of physical, emotional and mental limitations. Through Qigong I enliven my cells freeing up that which is physically, psychologically and spiritually dormant. The whitening of the embalming process also represents the spiritualization of the body or the physical made spiritual in our lives. In the Judgment card the spiritual awakening is illustrated with ashen colored people rising out of their stone coffins. Like the legendary Phoenix they are reborn anew in spiritual bodies that rise upwards to the spiritual world. The Judgment card marks the completion of the Lesser Work and the Resurrection of the *yin* soul. Redeemed, the *yin* soul seeks to reunite with the divine through the *yang* or *hun* evolutionary soul of the East, depicted here as an angel.

That the coffins float upon a sea of water seems very significant to me. Soul work is not an intellectual process. It is through working with the Dreamtime and the collective unconscious that the soul within the physical body is cleansed and made holy. Spiral Qigong is a purifying agent with dreams an important means of feedback so we can gauge our progress on the spiritual journey home. The following dream imagery and dialogue shows a serial progression in the self healing process.

> *Dream 22: Sleeping in a hotel room overlooking Lake Titicaca in Bolivia one morning, I dream of a blue stone under the earth. As I hold the stone and see myself dance with it, it begins to sing releasing swirling colored rainbow lights.*

I had a number of dreams about blue stones cluing me in to their significance. The first time the stone appeared during my Qigong practice, it looked sickly. As I focused my intention to connect energetically with it, my spontaneous movements changed to purge and then regenerate the stone. After several minutes the stone seemed to transform to a healthy state. As a dream symbol I felt the stone represented the state of my metal energy, the *yin po* body soul.

Several months later while touring Australia, I saw the blue stone again in a lucid state; only now it had a streak of red light shining from within that reminded me of the fiery opals native to Australia. The blue stone kept coming to mind during our travels

Down Under. I later found and bought a blue opal at the gift store while sightseeing some of the underground caves of Western Australia. Pondered as I gazed upon the stone I felt the red color represented the heating up or enlivening of my *po* body soul.

A few days later, while trying to sleep in Central Australia, I had the sense that the blue stone was moving up my Central Channel and into my heart. Having spent my younger years in Australia, I wondered if perhaps by returning to the place of my youth I was reconnecting with a dissociated part of myself. I believe we begin shutting down aspects of who we really are at an early age, particularly our intuitive dreaming abilities. Due to the malleability of our brain and body, when neural pathways are left unused they begin to shut down. The loss of our instincts and creative interplay with dreams is an unfortunate consequence of growing up in a western or left brain dominant culture.

In many native cultures where intuition and dreaming are valued, shamanic soul retrieval is performed as a healing practice by a qualified shaman. He or she typically journeys in a dream-like state to the lower or inner world to find and retrieve the fractured aspects of the soul that may have been separated by past traumas or disempowering events. These soul pieces are brought back into temporal time to be reincorporated into the client's body. Commonly shamans report finding lost soul pieces within caves during dream journeys. Such soul pieces having been found within the earth's mineral structure would represent the *po* body soul according to the inner traditions of Qigong.

Shamanic soul retrieval is often facilitated by the repetitive beating of a drum. The drum beat helps the shamanic practitioner get into a receptive state of mind to enter and change the dream experience. The drumming also mimics the heartbeat of the earth helping locate and free up those dormant and entrenched subterranean aspects of our souls. In shamanic training soul pieces are reincorporated by blowing them into the body, often into the area of the heart. Qigong became the source of my own unintended soul retrieval. The light blue stone in my lucid dream, representative of my *po* body soul, entered my body through the metal gate of CV-1. From there it naturally ascended via the Central Channel into the heart space at the middle *dan tian,* the spiritual adobe of the soul and place where *shen* and *ling* reunite.

In the Judgment card, the Western angel is a celestial counterpart to Chinese dragons. The angel in this card appears encircled by the clouds from what we can see. There are also spirals in the clouds to reinforce the transcendental symbolism. Like a fire breathing dragon (fire is the element of the heart), the angel blows spiritual breath through a golden trumpet in a sound healing practice similar to drumming induced shamanic soul retrieval. The action awakens the previously entombed people, symbols of disconnected soul pieces now returning, who rise upwards in celebration. The trumpet in the Judgment card is marked by a red cross on a white banner. This is an ancient alchemical sign from Asia of the union of *yin* and *yang* opposites.[17] Red *ling* (*yin* Spirit) and white *shen* (*yang* Spirit) come together in the heart. The trumpet being a hollow instrument is like the Central Channel. Connected to heaven and earth it is filled with transcendental central *qi.* In this card the severed aspects of the *po* body soul are waking from within the earth like central *qi* rising. They move upwards seeking divine union. In the Judgment card six people rise towards the seventh figure, the heavenly quality of the joyful heart.

Angels are often association with music making. This photo was taken from a sarcophagus at the Ephesus Museum in Turkey.

The stone was singing in dream 22. Singing is the sound associated with the heart in Chinese Medicine. The voice, like the trumpet in the Judgment card, is a wind instrument and carrier of God's word. The dream likewise shows the perfection of the *po* body soul through the rainbow light emitted from the stone. A rainbow appears when divine white light is refracted through a crystal prism. The alchemical dreams show purification of the metal element over time. Through spiritual transformation the base metals of my nature have been refined with the *po* soul becoming more wholesome as the stone appears healthier and more colorful. Fully awakened the stone now emanates all seven colors of the rainbow, reflecting a level of incorruptibility according to different traditions. Here we find the creation of the Philosopher's Stone, an alternate name for the Holy Grail. The immortal golden body of Taoist alchemists is also called the spiritual body of rainbow light to Western Gnostic traditions. The rainbow colors also reflect the rainbow body or body of light, the highest spiritual level of the physical body in Tibetan Buddhism.

> Dream 23: *I see our property in Eastern Washington, dry land with patches of prairie grass. From my mind's eye, I watch as the earth suddenly cracks open and a gigantic blue snake emerges from within. As it slithers upon the ground, I see that it is covered in African tribal symbols with five circular markings upon the upper edge of the forehead. Once the snake leaves, the crack in the earth closes and reseals.*

The transcendental spiritual force of central *qi* is released from the earth when *yin* and *yang* reunite. The blue snake coming out of the burial ground of the earth is a symbol of the awakening global spiritual energy along channels called dragon lines in China or fairy paths in Ireland. The blue fairy under the water in dream 8 may have hinted at this enlivened spiritual energy within the planet as well. Harmonizing *yin* and *yang* within the body, we can develop the ability to unlock latent spiritual energies within matter and the planet Earth. The Chinese, as we have discussed, harmonize elements of the landscape using the ancient art of *feng shui,* translated as wind water, an aspect of geomancy. Australian Aborigines maintain the timeless connection to the sacred Dreamtime through ceremonial walking and singing (like the singing rock in my dream) along special paths of sacred locations. Walking the ancestral tracks, they maintain the mythical or spiritual dimension of the physical land they have responsibility to care for. Dragon lines have different *yin* and *yang* polarities; however, dragon lairs are spiraling vortexes of energy creating etheric pillars of light between earth and heaven.[5] These vortexes of energy are channels for Christ consciousness as later dreams have shown. Working to activate and use the transcendental central *qi* of our physical environment, we have the ability to facilitate spiritual ascension and intuitive dreaming on a larger scale.

In ancient Egypt, the pyramids unified heaven and earth creating vortexes of energy. Doing Qigong on our land in Eastern Washington, I have seen the blue energy rising from beneath the

Jesus pulling Adam and Eve out of hell and into heaven following the Resurrection. This religious scene is on the wall of the Chora Church in Istanbul, Turkey.

ground, depicting the celestial energies released from matter. I have also felt the physical spiraling movements of the vortexes standing over them. I should not be surprised as the blue serpent rising out of the earth in dream 23 foretold of this.

The serpent represents the path of consciousness to the Mayan culture. The main pyramid at Chichen Itza, Mexico and the Temple of the Grand Jaguar in Tikal, Guatemala depict cosmic serpents.

Section B:

The Virtues of *Yang*

Chapter 16

The Tower

Dream 24: I have a bird's eye view of the Statue of Liberty, up close focusing on her head and torch.

Completing the Lesser Work of inner alchemy, my dreams shifted to address the *yang* or masculine side of spiritual development. Symbols of feminine water energies are replaced by those of fire, such as the upheld torch of the Statue of Liberty. Fire represents *shen* and the south pole of the vertical axis mundi. It symbolizes the Central Sun, the eternal timeless dimension of the Tao or the Dreamtime. Beyond dualistic concepts of masculine and feminine, this *yang* aspect of the divine can be associated with the Father God figure of the Judaic, Christian and Muslim traditions. According to Chinese Medicine theory, *shen* is accessible to each of us and stored in the upper *dan tian* of the head. Described qualitatively as lightening and thunder[39], this etheric energy enters the body through acupoint GV-20 at the apex of the head. As we build the quantity of *shen* in the upper *dan tian* we refine the power of the conscious mind and our abilities to unite with Spirit.

The Statue of Liberty's official name when translated from French means 'Liberty Enlightening the World'.[40] Dream 24 teaches that the *yin* soul of the metal element has been liberated and moved upwards to unite and integrate with the *yang* soul. The green color of Lady Liberty shows the acquisition of wood element characteristics. Her coppery greenness links her to spiritual rebirth of the east. The Liberty statue, like that of the Tower card, is also of tremendous height. Having been freed, the energies of the soul reach upwards into the heavens. Upon the

Liberty's head, seven rays of light are shown emanating from her crown. Having resolved detrimental subconscious tendencies, purging the seven emotions from the body, I have built a foundation to now build *shen* spiritual energies. The crown of spiritual illumination shows my growing spiritual connection. I have greater awareness of and can more easily follow the spiritual light that guides me through dreaming.

Shen fire descends to earth in the Tower card as cosmic rays of light. This heavenly energy, as lightening, strikes or enters the top of the tower image. The tower is simply a metaphor for the Central Channel of the body. The Tower card depicts *yang* Spirit entering the Central Channel through GV-20 at the top of the head. A similar dream of mine showed a Buddhist bust with a burning candle at from this acupoint. I would later learn that this Ushnisha or 'flame of invisible light' is a sacred symbol of divine intelligence in Buddhist and Christian scriptures. Like the golden crown in the Tower card, the Ushnisha represents a holy or enlightened individual.[2]

Lady Liberty holds the light of illumination for others to follow to safety in New York, USA. The statue was created by French Freemasons.

Dream 25: Traveling by plane, I sit in the back of the aircraft on the left. While flying, a stewardess moves me to a seat in the right upper midsection of the plane. My seat is directly behind the toilets now rather than a long way off. I think how fortunate as it will be much easier to go to the bathroom from this new location.

Initially with Spiral Qigong, a great deal of the healing work is very body-oriented. Spontaneous movements strongly move and purge the body, freeing up densities within the energy channels and the cells of the body. Muscles and organs holding past tensions also physically contract and CV-1 naturally vibrates to channel in healthy life force energies to facilitate this work. In the Greater Work of alchemy, the conscious mind, having been strengthened through regular Qigong practice, takes an ever greater role in healing. Using the mind's eye, we can efficiently use the power of intention to transmute low density energies.

In my dream, the movement forward in the plane makes going to the bathroom easier. I have an easier time accessing the toilet, an instrument used to cleanse the body of toxins. The purging of the upper *dan tian* in the center of the brain is shown in the Tower card with the flames burning in the upper window and the top of the structure. Here the removal of dualistic concepts of *yin* and *yang* are illustrated by the falling man and woman. With them goes exclusivity and ideas of good and bad or right and wrong that interfere with our union with Spirit.

The movement to the right in dream 25 shows a shift of focus

Glastonbury Tor, England; a location associated with St Michael and thought to be a major center for dragon ley lines or energy currents within the earth. Glastonbury Tor rests upon a large spiral mound and is a site associated with mythical Avalon where the dead are guided to eternal life.

from the *yin* to the *yang* soul. This is where the removal of attachments, anger and resentments moves us forward in oneness consciousness. Eradicating egotistical filters and judgments, the lower windows or eyes of the Tower become clean. The eyes are the sensory organs of the *yang* soul. Removing the veils of separation, the eyes return to their natural luminosity and sparkle with inner fire. Reflecting the divine light of Spirit, the eyes in Chinese Medicine are the windows of the soul.

> *Dream 26: Walking south along the highway, I cross the bridge over the Columbia River and into Portland, Oregon. We are in a time of war and I look and feel serious and concerned as I approach downtown Portland. I see the buildings in front of me and know that if twelve bombs go off that everything will be fine. With bated breath, I intently watch the buildings counting the eleventh and then the twelfth and final explosion. I sigh, feeling a sudden wave of relief. I then turn around and begin walking home. I pass people along the way who are joyfully celebrating this new era of peace.*

I had the above sleeping dream after learning that my father, who had been working as a construction engineer in Iraq, was a hostage. This had been confirmed to me when earlier in the day I sat watching my father on CNN, head shaven and badly beaten with machine guns pointing to the sides of his head asking the United States and Australian governments to withdraw troops from Iraq. The message was clear: Remove foreign occupancy or my dad would be killed.

I felt upon waking from dream 26 that I had been given a message that my dad would be all right though certain events, signified by the succession of bombs, were needed before things would resolve. I somehow felt that I was being tested, and that I needed to be extremely mindful of my thoughts and actions during the time ahead. Everything, big or small, was significant and could potentially affect the results of this tenuous situation.

Looking back upon the dream years later, I suspect archetypal significance behind the dream as well. Moving to the south, I walked towards the element of fire and the indestructible transcendence of God. Crossing the bridge, I passed a threshold into the timeless dimension of the collective unconscious. The number twelve, like the hands of a clock, represent the circular path of the Ouroborus. There are twelve astrological signs in the zodiac, twelve disciples around Jesus, twelve trigrams in the I Ching, twelve stones in a Native American medicine wheel, twelve tribes of Israel and twelve gates to the alchemical manufacture of gold and immortality. There are twelve numbers on a clock and twelve months to the year, showing this number as a symbol of the dimensions of time and space. Going around the periphery, we complete the circle and become whole ourselves. As dream 26 shows, when we heal ourselves, the consciousness of the planet evolves as well.

Dream 27: Receiving a massage, I begin to lucid dream. I am aware of being in the jungles of South America. I feel a lot of fear and chaos energy there and have a sense of people I care about being hurt beyond my control. Glancing upwards, I see an etheric image of myself high above the massage table looking serenely through a small triangle watching the crazy jungle scene below. I keep my attention above the triangle as the scene of pain and loss plays out. Being unattached from this higher perspective, I am able to clear and release the situation. Releasing the nightmarish scene, I also let go of a long held pain in the right side of my chest.

This lucid dream experience was induced while I was relaxed and receiving bodywork. Here I learned to disengage from an emotionally charged trauma by keeping my consciousness above the triangle and the dream situation. The triangle of my dream, like the windows of the Tower card, represent the Trinity aspect of the Tao. Through the reunion of physical (*jing*), emotional (*qi*) and spiritual (*shen*) within the Central Channel, I am given a tool to transcend the situation. Whether this dream experience was symbolic or literal, doesn't really matter. The important point is that I was able to consciously forgive and release any perceived injustices and hurt to or from myself. Maintaining a presence on the eternal side of the gateway, shown here as above the triangle, high frequency *shen* energies helped me release the root issue and replace the former pain with a what I experienced as a warm infusion in the chest and a great sense of peace. After this intense healing event I was happy to note that I no longer had the subconscious need to attract discordant energy released by my clients in treatment sessions. This problem of picking up other people's energetic pain and stress is something I had noted and been concerned about since my student days at OCOM. By subconsciously holding the painful experience within my body I was attracting similar low vibrations to me. Taking responsibility for what I attracted into my life I then chose to release the root trauma and resolve the issue from the inside out.

Dream 27 reminded me of the movie *Clash of the Titans*. I saw this movie in a theater as a young kid when I was growing up in California. In the movie, the gods watched and effortlessly influenced the world of mortals from high atop Mount Olympus. Homer similarly depicted the gods influencing and affecting people and events in *The Iliad* and *The Odyssey*. My lucid dream experience shows we all have an aspect of ourselves in this realm of infinite possibility. Connecting with the spiritual aspect of ourselves, we can promptly clear ourselves. Abundance, good health and a state of peace will naturally unfold afterwards. We can perhaps achieve more by being in the Dreamtime than by doing in our physical dimension, though this is sometimes difficult to intellectually comprehend. We are all magicians, however, who can work with the state of the infinite to reach our goals.

Chapter 17

The Hierophant

Dream 28: From the open mouth of a green wine bottle, I see wine pouring. It collects in a crystal goblet below.
Dream 29: The image of a tall clear cylindrical drinking glass filled with red berry juice followed by the image of a vertical oriented rainbow colored snake.

The alchemical books describe two primary stages: *the white work* and *the red work.*[41] The High Priestess of the tarot represents the 'White Queen' and the Lesser Works of alchemy. Here in this card the Hierophant as the 'Red King' represents the Great Works of alchemy. In this phase called *Rubedo,* the union of soul and Spirit is achieved.[41]

A clay sculpture dating back 8,500 years, found at the Catal Huyuk archeological site in modern day Turkey, shows the Great Mother sitting upon her throne. She is the earliest artistic image of a person upon a throne. Thereafter, according to author, scholar and artist, Lydia Ruyle, thrones themselves represent the mother in many cultures. Thousands of years later the Egyptian Goddess Isis was the throne of Osiris, as reflected in the hieroglyphs for Isis and illustrations of her in temples throughout Egypt. She wears upon her head the triple-stepped ladder, just as the Hierophant wears the triple-layered crown. The High Priestess and that which she represents is likewise the foundation of the Hierophant. Symbolized as a throne in this card she marks the importance of purifying the subconscious mind and the body in becoming a spiritualized individual. Neglecting to do the inner work, the consciousness of the body will eventually rebel despite the best intentions and spiritual aspirations of the conscious mind.

In the Star card, we discussed how the Central Channel called Chong Mai is more accurately translated as Central Blood Vessel. Aligning the three *dan tian*, also known as the internal treasures, it is this channel that holds the keys to esoteric wisdom. Here we can create the alchemical elixir or cinnabar field by internal cultivation techniques like Qigong. Like the red outer robe of the Hierophant, cinnabar is a red colored alchemical substance that symbolizes the flow of Spirit. The red clothing upon the Hierophant make him look like a woman from China in traditional attire on her wedding day. There, the red color represents joy, love and prosperity for the uniting couple.

Red colored fluids such as blood and wine are metaphors for the union of soul and Spirit.

In dream 28, spiritual energies are depicted as red wine. Wine is a substitute for divine blood in the Dionysian Greek Mysteries as well in the Catholic Holy Communion. Pope John XXIII proclaimed in *The Precious Blood of Jesus* that mankind was redeemed by the shedding of Jesus' blood.[42] The historical sacredness of blood is evident in Paleolithic archeological artifacts over 20,000 years old. Objects of sacred value were consecrated and made holy with blood or a blood substitute.[23] Likewise, when Jesus 'transmutes' water into wine at the wedding of Canaan, the Bible may be alluding to the alchemical union of *yin* and *yang* energies within the body. In my dream, the wine pours forth from the circular opening of the green wine bottle. The Ouroborus circle is once again the symbol for the gateway to access the dimension beyond time and space.

The green coloring of the glass bottle brings to mind the most significant contribution to Western European alchemy – the Emerald Tablet. The Emerald Tablet is an alchemical text written on emerald stone. It was allegedly found in the tomb of Hermes Trismegistus, a priest believed to have introduced alchemy into Egypt. The writings of this text include these lines:

Its power is perfect....With great sagacity it ascends gently from Earth to heaven, and it descends again to Earth, uniting in itself the forces above and from below. Thus you will possess the glory of the brightness of the whole world, and all obscurities will fly from you.

Interestingly, the Emerald Text describes the cultivation technique of Spiral Qigong described in Part II. The glory of the brightness of the whole world would be the spiritualized matter resulting when heaven and earth unite to create the transcendental spiraling force of central *qi*.

In Chapter 9 a sequence of dreams with bowls and vases collecting water was described. Dream 28 shows a subtle yet significant variation. The collection of flowing energies occurs high atop a glass stem rather than upon the ground itself. The long stem is a metaphor for the Central Channel. The upper collecting bowl of the goblet shows that the upper *dan tian* in the head is building a healthy supply of spiritual energies. The more we fill this sacred vessel the better we can see and focus our mental thoughts on the spiritual nature of our existence. Cerebral focus as a means to spiritual enlightenment is in the Hierophant card as well. The ram-like head engravings high upon the pillars are one example. The tops of their heads are intentionally left open to show access to divine celestial energies through GV-20. The massive golden crown upon the head of the Hierophant, along with the triple cross at the apex of the golden staff, also highlight the spiritual significance of storing *shen qi* in the upper *dan tian*.

The crystal drinking vessels in dream 28 can be compared to the red sack atop the wooden pole of the Fool card. Both are a symbol of the Holy Grail. Holy Grail stories of myth and lore promise food, wealth and fertility to the knight who obtains it.[42] Creating something from nothing is a benefit of working with the Tao as shown by the Magician. Using intention (*shen*) with spiritual potency (*ling*), we move downward along the manifestation cycle to create the cornucopia or horn of plenty. Animal horns are spiraling energies of the head. They demonstrate the importance of intention to a spiritual adept in harmonizing energies to help generate abundance and fertility for all.

The cylindrical vessel in dream 29 depicts the entire Central Channel and body as being transparent or clear of obstruction. Filled with red liquid, it is similar to the Hierophant depicted in Waite's tarot card. Lower, middle and upper *dan tian* have been strengthened and synchronized. Spirit as red juice now flows uninterrupted throughout this central axis. Dream 29 also shows the Central Channel depicted as a vertically aligned and upright rainbow colored snake. Here is the ancestral Rainbow Serpent of Australia and the keeper of the aboriginal Dreamtime. The wisdom of the body is the collective unconscious. It is the electromagnetic spectrum of light demonstrating the full flow of universal energies. Purified, our bodies become crystal prisms refracting the pure light of consciousness into the seven colors of the rainbow.

A lone vertical rising serpent petroglyph is found at the heart of the Incan Empire in Cusco, Peru. Former Director of the National Institute of Culture, Dr. Jose (Pepe) Altamirano, teaches how the Incan's connected with the serpent of the lower world through dance and movement like kundalini practices of the East.

The Hierophant is an individual imbued with spiritual potential and aware of the presence of God. The white vertical line upon the Hierophant's red robe depicts three crosses.

Author dreams of the Australian Aboriginal Rainbow Serpent Mother during a visit to Australia. A similar Rainbow Goddess is honored in Africa, Cuba, Haiti and Puerto Rico.

Representing the three *dan tian* of ancient Chinese philosophy, it shows the balance of the physical, emotional and spiritual within the individual. The importance of this Trinity in creating the immortal golden body is shown by the golden three-tiered crown upon his head and the triple-cross staff, reflecting his control of the three worlds. The staff appears grounded, resting upon the earth behind the Hierophant's back. Like Taoist thought, the lower tier is emphasized in size, as physical vitality is the foundation of spiritual ascension. A subtle diamond shape is seen at the bottom of the white vertical stripe. Literally meaning 'world goddess', the diamond replaced the tarot's pentacle suit in modern playing cards.[13] As a feminine symbol of earth energies, it also represents the enlivened CV-1 of the spiritual adept.

The Hierophant's head is above the reservoir of spiritual energies. The white stripe on the Hierophant's shoulders marks the collecting vessel of the upper dan tian. When viewed from above the white stripe also forms the circular shape of the Ouroborus. Its meaning is equal to the triangle as threshold to heavenly energies of my earlier dream. Transcendental oneness is known consciously since the head of the Hierophant is above the circular form.

The Hierophant as spiritual adept has integrated the spiritual in physical form: the two complementary opposites of *yin* and *yang* pictured as twin monks with Y upon their backs are the *yang* soul (greenery upon clothing) and *yin* soul (white flowers upon attire). Raised one step above the others, the Hierophant exists in a plane of higher consciousness harmonizing these principles as one. The Hierophant is privy to the golden secrets of all life. He or she channels down the energies of heaven through the upward-turned right hand. This relaxed hand position, entitled 'sword fingers' in Qigong, is a way to direct heavenly energies into physical reality.

Creating the elixir of life, the individual as well as the physical world benefit.[3] In the Hierophant card, the red color of Spirit cascades down the Hierophant's robes spreading upon the carpet below. Physical matter becomes spiritualized and rises from below as shown by the blue undergarments above the feet and around the Hierophant's neck. Like the Hindu god Shiva, described in Chapter 13, the blue color of heaven at the neck demonstrates the individual's ability to transmute the poisons of the world.

In Wolfram von Eschenbach's Arthurian tale *Parzival,* he uses alchemical imagery of the black and white checkerboard to describe the union of *yin* and *yang* opposites.[3] Checkered lines on the carpet of the Hierophant depict the spiraling dragon lines of central *qi* flowing within the earth. Originating from this spiritual figurehead, as well as the emptiness of the Tao in the background, two streams lead to the junior monks who have shaved heads centered around acupoint GV-20. Like the offering of Jesus' wine to the guests at the wedding of Canaan, this symbolizes a means of transmitting spiritual knowledge and initiating others. The drinking of wine continues to be a spiritual ritual to identify and unite with Jesus Christ as one.[43]

The X is an early symbol for the Christ.[44] In the Hierophant card there are white X's upon the shoes of the Hierophant and upon the ground. The X symbol represents Christ consciousness energy. When heaven and earth unite in a spiritual adept, the spiritual energy of the heavens unites and balances the earthly forces of nature. The energies of the four directions, specifically the elements of wood, fire, water and metal, come together towards the central point, represented by the earth element. Together they form the shape of an equidistant cross. Rising upwards from the center, the Christ consciousness energy, the Christian term for central *qi,* is unlocked. The Hierophant card teaches that by actively working to awaken the flow of Christ consciousness energy within the earth we can raise the vibrational field of the planet and bring heaven to earth. Like the Hierophant, Chinese Emperors of the past maintained peace and order in their kingdom through such inner cultivation techniques. Working to harmonize the energies of ourselves and the earth, we increase spiritual potency to heal others and the world.

> *Dream 30: I see my grandfather who died almost fifteen years earlier beside me. He is smiling upon me and supporting my authentic spiritual expression. I feel his love and pride in me.*

During a Sunday service before Christmas 2007 while singing Christmas hymns, I was moved to tears by the beauty of the overall experience. Singing songs like *Joy to the World* and *Ave Maria,* I was deeply touched by the sacredness of the event we were honoring. I sang and cried freely with an open heart in supportive communion. It was during this church service that my paternal grandfather appeared to me through conscious dreaming. As the Moderator General of the Presbyterian Church of Australia, my grandfather was a real life hierophant to me and many others.

Growing up on the other side of the world in the United States and away from my grandfather's religious influence, my parents and I seldom went to church. We usually only attended Sunday service during my grandparents' annual visit. I loved my grandfather and fondly remember drawing biblical images and scenes from the Good News Bible in my letters to him. He included similar sketches by hand in his postings. It was our own special ritual and a way to connect. I also fondly gazed upon the angel statuettes he gave me when I was young and loved the gentle figure of Saint Francis of Assisi in my parents' room. Despite these fond memories and affections, I felt alienated from my family's Christian heritage as an adult. Yearning to deepen my Christian spiritual connection, I tried numerous times to read the Bible. More often than not, however, I came to a passage that denigrated women or spoke of a wrathful, judging God and, feeling disappointed, I would abruptly stop reading. I could not embrace a spiritual tradition based upon fear and anti-feminine principles. Disconnected and dissatisfied, I needed, as part of my spiritual journey, to clear my prejudices and sense of separation from my spiritual ancestry. I felt compelled to establish an authentic relationship with the divine father and find peace with Christianity.

During the second half of my spiritual awakening, my dreams took a very *yang* archetypal theme. Images of patriarchal god figures of Greek, Egyptian, Native American and Incan cultures were common in addition to dream images of the sun, fire and Michelangelo's *The Creation of Adam* artwork from the ceiling of the Sistine Chapel in Rome. Though this shift was unexpected, the balance of feminine and masculine forces felt logically appropriate. It was now a period of Dreamtime synchronizing with the eternal and timeless aspect of the masculine face of God.

Christian scholar Elaine Pagels, Ph.D. shares insights into Christian scriptures in her audio book *The Gospel of Thomas: New Perspectives on Jesus' Message*. Pagels notes how Jesus' teachings were likely influenced by Eastern traditions. Pagels believes the little known *Gospel of Thomas* offered high level spiritual guidance for initiates seeking to attain the divinity of Jesus. The Apostle Thomas known as 'Doubting Thomas' taught the appropriateness of discernment and spiritual insight achieved through direct experience. Dreams and experiences of Mother Mary, Jesus and Mary Magdalene have led me to explore and deepen my Christian connection and embrace Christ more fully. Returning home to my spiritual religious faith that day in church, I experienced new found joy and acceptance in the loving presence of my grandfather.

Despite Michelangelo's painting of a paternal god, Pope John Paul II's 1999 Easter Sunday address reminds us that 'The Law of the Old Testament explicitly forbids representation of the invisible and ineffable God by means of "graven or molten image" (*Deut.* 27:15), because God transcends every material representation'. Beyond gender and form or *yin* and *yang* distinction, the Heavenly Father is comparable to the undifferentiated Tao. The transcendental Spirit is infinite and eternal. It is only to better comprehend, understand and connect that we have, through the ages, sought to make God tangible and in so doing defined as gender specific and often masculine.

Dream 31: I am talking with a ceremonially dressed papal figure describing my beliefs about the body soul connection. He listens respectfully then nods his head in agreement, telling me I am correct. I wake in the morning to a word: Assumption.

I have always loved visiting places of worship wherever I live and travel. Entering Catholic churches and cathedrals throughout France, Italy, Germany, Egypt, Bolivia, Peru and Turkey, I experienced a sense of the sacred. Waking up from dream 31, I was not aware of the meaning of the word *Assumption* though it seemed to have a link to Catholicism and Jesus. Following the dream, I referred to my son's *Illustrated World Encyclopedia*. It described how the 'Assumption' occurred when the Virgin Mary died and was transported to heaven with her body and soul united. Catholic belief in the Assumption goes back 1,500 years though it was only made official by the Roman Catholic Church in 1950 by Pope Pius XII.[45]

In August 15, 2004, Pope John Paul II quoted John 14:3 of the Bible to explain the Assumption of Mary. At the Last Supper, Jesus explained, 'When I go and prepare a place for you, I will come again and will take you to myself, that where I am, there you may be also'. Jesus, following the Resurrection, was taken body and soul into heaven. As a savior figure, Jesus is the Christian way to everlasting life through union with God.

The Hierophant in dream 31 shows Catholic dogma regarding eternal life as analogous with Taoist thought. The union of body (*po* or body soul) and soul (*hun* or evolutionary soul) is another way of understanding the Assumption of Mary. Pope John Paul II's words remind us that through unity with Jesus, we can likewise all be one in heaven. Whatever spiritual tradition we follow, each of us has the potential to achieve this state of transcendental awareness and find everlasting life. Qigong Dreaming, as I have been told, can be a primary tool to help reach this state of grace.

Chapter 18

The Lovers

> *Dream 32: I see myself sitting atop the branches of a tree eating golden apples. Barefoot, I playfully swing my feet and watch the plants that I am helping grow on the earth around the tree. A snake comes up the tree trunk to visit, then descends again.*

In the Lovers card, we have female and male opposites together again. No longer do they wear self-imposed chains and restrictions around their necks as they did in the Devil card. Here they are unencumbered by clothing and without judgment or fear of their nakedness. The trees behind the male and female figures show that both have symbolically returned to the euphoric Garden of Eden. The snake to the left has climbed back up the tree of life to reunite with the primordial Tao. Aligned with earth and heaven, the woman has the inner awareness (*you*) and sees the angelic presence above her.

The above dream shows that in ascending the tree, I have also freed the creative potentials buried in my subconscious body. Moving my legs spontaneously as I do in Qigong, I have reconnected with my childlike playfulness. Without conscious effort I watch and help the plants grow around me in the dream. When

> The Australiana Tree on the top of Mount Dandenong near Melbourne, Australia shows a snake spiraling upwards in a counterclockwise direction to the apex. The wooden artwork is similar to indigenous totem poles in China and along the West coast of Canada and USA. The wooden totem can be symbolic of the human body.

we let go and move authentically in Qigong we like the ancient Chinese alchemists ground spiritual energies into the earth. Increased order and harmony within the energy channels of the planet translates as increased fertility and abundance around us.

Allowing the cyclical flow of energy within the microcosmic orbit, represented by ascending and descending snake symbolism, is a way to be a constructive force in the universe. In the Lovers card, the serpent coils around the tree three and a half times, the same number as a bronze serpent artifact from 1027 to 255 BCE China.[46] This earliest archeological evidence of the spiral suggests that China had knowledge of working with the transcendental central *qi* for healing that later spread to India and developed to be known as kundalini in tantric yoga.[28] Similar coiled serpent artifacts from around 50 CE have been found in Rome and suggest comparable practices throughout all of Eurasia.[28]

Why does the serpent rotate three and a half turns? From an ancient Chinese perspective, this represents the awakening of the three *dan tian*. Once the lower, middle and upper centers have been purified, the central *qi* rises a half step from the center of the head to acupoint GV-20 at the crown. This is the place also associated with the seventh chakra *Sahasrara* where the individual experiences union with the transcendental. The serpent in the tree of the Lover's card rises from the earth in a counterclockwise direction. The spiral similarly flows counter-clockwise in the Magician and the Wheel of Fortune cards, as unlocking this energy from matter is the key to physical, emotional and spiritual health.

Dream 33: I am driving through Eastern Washington with my husband seated to my right. Looking to the right I notice a tall dried out wood snag. Continuing onward, I reach out and interlock my arm with my husband's.

Wood in Chinese Medicine corresponds to the liver and gall bladder, organs located under the rib cage on the right side of the body. The liver is known in Chinese theory to be the planner and visionary of the body. This major organ maintains the big picture and the overall goal while the gall bladder is responsible for taking the step by step actions to accomplish the directives set by the liver. Both organs work together to ensure the healthy smooth flow of the *qi* and creativeness of the individual. Stress, resentments, anger and repressed creativity are all conditions that disrupt and stagnate the flow of energy in the body. Stagnation may also lead to areas of pain and discomfort. Due to our hectic lifestyle and cultural conformity, a diagnosis of liver stagnation is common for people living in Western cultures.

Considering the dead wood snag in dream 33, I first looked at my endeavors to see if I was inappropriately expending energies in my life as the wood organs are on the right side of the body. The gall bladder in particular is a *yang* or masculine organ relating to the right. My vision was to teach Spiral Qigong as a holistic wellness practice and help people connect with their dreaming. Perhaps my dream was hinting at a need to readjust my actions in reaching this goal. Following dream 33, I chose to take a temporary break from teaching evening classes so I could focus instead on teaching through my writings. It was spring when I had the dream, a particularly potent time to do some internal spring cleaning. Letting go of certain time requirements allowed space for other activities that my soul yearned for and the creation of this book. Reaching out in the dream to the right and embracing my husband as a symbol of my masculine side, I know that in refocusing my *yang* wood energies I will come back into balance.

Dreaming about dried wood in dream 33 also confirmed that I had outdated energies from the past ready to be purged. A periodic stuck pressure in the right hand side of my ribcage showed a liver imbalance. Acupuncture and herbal medicine only gave temporary relief, and though my liver enzymes were normal, I knew that on a more subtle level there was healing to be done. There was tending to do to my metaphorical garden. In the generating cycle of energy in the body, wood nourishes and feeds fire. Burning away old wood related issues and repressed emotions purifies the *yang* soul and nourishes our spiritual development.

When issues surface consciously through dreams and body experiences or I just feel off emotionally, I use a powerful Qigong Dreaming technique with the Ouroborus symbol. Letting go of my attachment to the specific item, I direct it out of my body and visualize it as a dream image in front of me. I next create an Ouroborus above me with my mind's intention. The O shaped spiral becomes a portal that vacuums up the lower vibrational energies into the central void. The stuck emotion, belief, thought, or body symptom is, therefore, returned to the undifferentiated state of pure Source. I use this purification technique for releasing the energetic fingerprint behind nightmares and discordant emotional states within myself and clients. Handing the issue over to God, one can quickly remove low frequency thoughts and emotions; doing so we create space for greater flow and consciousness in life.

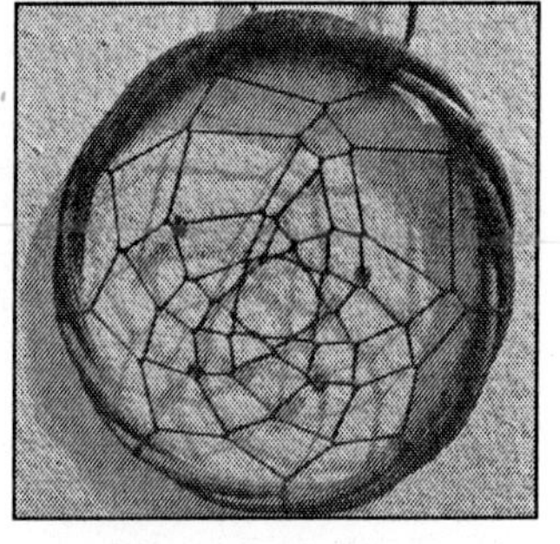

The Native American dream catcher shows a spiral web that catches unwanted nightmares. The central circular opening allows the good dreams to flow to the dreamer.

Similarly, in the Lovers card, we find the wood burning as a tree on the right hand side behind the male figure. Unwanted impurities are burned away rising upwards towards the angelic being with fire-like hair. Fire is a spiritual force for heating the body and transcending all densities. Purging our mind-body we become empty or void ourselves. Maintaining emptiness (wu) there is an aspect of ourselves that remains neutral through life's changes, like the impartial gaze of the man in this card. He has released judgments and attachments to a higher power seen above but actually within himself. Using mental faculties and the energy of intention from the upper *dan tian* he uses fire to transmute and transcend thoughts of separation making room for spiritual union.

> *Dream 34a: A bride and groom are together outside a church following their wedding. The bride is relieved that the man she has just married had returned from his ordeals, initiations she placed for him to face, and is back home safe and sound.*

The divine feminine qualities of dreaming and Qigong body movement facilitated my physical, emotional and spiritual growth just as the bride in the above dream initiated her husband. Taoist philosophy views the challenges we face as the will of heaven. All events whether waking or dreaming are heaven's attempt to nourish our innate potential.[12] Closing off authentic self-expression, we obstruct the flow of *qi* between heaven and earth within ourselves.[12] Peace of mind, health and joy may become elusive until we get back on track remembering our individual destiny. Guided through dreams, we face and overcome our individual challenges and mature as we learn virtues of compassion and benevolence. The marriage of bride and groom reflects the balance of *yin* and *yang* opposites as well as spiritual unity with a transcendental God. Through sacred marriage we return to our natural wholeness and inner bliss.

Applying *yin* and *yang* concepts to the biology of the human brain, we find that the woman and man in the Lovers card can correspond to the right and left hemispheres, respectively. Brain science researcher Dr. Jill Bolte Taylor explained the different functions of each side of the brain in *My Stroke of Insight: A Brain*

Scientist's Personal Experience. The right brain controls the left half of the body and represents feminine wisdom. It is the intuitive and instinctual thinking center. Here, without concept of time, we live in a euphoric presence of abundance. Right brain activity is conducive to feelings of interconnectedness and empathy for others. It is the side of the brain where gut feelings guide us. By using the right side of the brain more, we become more spontaneous and feel deep inner peace.

Lao Tzu focused on the importance of inner awareness. Body-minded awareness through Qigong movement meditation is one way to neurologically stimulate right brain activity and the timeless dimension of the Tao. Facilitating intuition and dreaming Qigong is a powerful tool for enhancing personal connection with Source. Through regular practice, Qigong is an effective means to develop peaceful mind, joyful heart and spiritual awareness.

> *Dream 34b: As the couple move to join the wedding reception, they see a man in front of them stuck in a box of burning fire that is closing down upon him. The angry man tells the couple that he wanted to kill the young groom but inadvertently trapped himself instead within the box of fire and is dying.*

Jill Bolte Taylor also described the function of the left brain in her book that chronicled the effects of a stroke to this left or masculine part of her brain. She described how the left brain processes information in a linear and literal fashion. It categorizes and orders events by past, present and future and breaks down concepts and patterns to understand them.[47] The left brain is the mind chatter of the ego. Here critical thoughts and judgments define our understanding of what is good and bad. Through the left brain we compare and contrast ourselves to others. Excessive left brain activity leads to feelings of dissatisfaction and stress about finances, work and relationships. It creates self doubt and promotes frailty, isolation and loneliness if not balanced with right brain activity.[47]

According to Dr. Kat Domingo we become enlightened through a process of unlearning.[47] To overcome dualistic thinking we need to let go of all the things we thought we knew. Letting go of resentments and the need to be right we are happier as well as healthier (for example anger increases risk of heart disease). Also, there is no room for Spirit when our minds and hearts are full of judgments and condemnation against ourselves and others. Employing body oriented techniques like Qigong we can reduce the left brain dominance which is the source of disease and discontentment. Lao Tzu referred to emptiness as the beginning of our spiritual unfolding. Releasing past judgments and attachments, the man in the burning box in dream 34b is my ego. My ego confesses to trying to kill off my spiritual side as represented by the male groom. Repressed angers and judgments have been released through Qigong Dreaming. With each release the ego's battle for control is weakened. Trapped and contained within the burning box the ego's destructive mind chatter is being burned away. I have successfully freed my authentic self from some self-imposed restrictions. Dream 34b confirmed the benefit of this baptism by fire on the journey to unity consciousness.

Western culture is heavily left brain focused and excessively *yang*. My sense is that a lot of the personal strife and social issues we face, including depression, abuse, addictions, mental health concerns, crime, environmental degradation and international conflict, stem from overactive left brain activity at the individual and collective levels. Feeling forsaken and victimized or alternately superior and justified in condemning others, we are literally East of Eden. Having unresolved wood element issues also keeps the body and mind vibrating at a lower state. Holding the energetic signature of past conflicts, anger, resentment, judgment and criticism, we attract those things into our lives. Taking responsibility we can do the inner alchemical work to transmute these road blocks and spiritual maturity. Developing the intuitive and instinctive nature of ourselves we are shown the way back into balance. Then we too can enjoy the golden fruit of Paradise as dream 32 indicates.

> *Dream 35: Seated on the right in a window seat of an airplane, I look out the window watching our approach to Uluru, formerly known as Ayers Rock, in the middle of Australia. Gazing tranquilly, I experience a lucid dream and see an image of myself, legs crossed and eyes closed, meditating high in the sky. I watch as my image transforms into Jesus Christ. It again shape shifts to become a shimmering and golden Holy Grail. The image changes once more into a middle-aged aboriginal woman purifying her womb through menstruation.*

Mountains are considered sacred places associated with increased intuition and receptivity. In China, the Immortals are depicted in dreamlike settings high atop the mountains and among the clouds. In places without natural mountains, people created temples, pyramids and megalithic structures of stone to facilitate spiritual awareness. Likewise, many myths associate sacred dreaming with the element of metal. Jacob in the Old Testament falls asleep with a rock under his head and has a vision of angels ascending and descending a spiral staircase. Moses climbed a mountain to receive the word of God and returned with the Ten Commandments. Muslims around the world honor spiritual pilgrimage to Mecca where the holy of holies centers upon a black stone. The great pyramids of Giza were likely used for spiritual initiation and ascension. Ancient temples to the sun god Apollo in current day Greece and Turkey were centers of oracular knowledge and dream cultivation. Catholic churches around the world have a reputation for inducing visions of the Virgin Mother.

I had been to Egypt a few months before my travels to Australia and had experienced first hand increased dreaming from my proximity to ancient sacred sites. Our hotel in Cairo was within short walking distance to the pyramids. In fact, I could see one of the pyramids from the hotel grounds. Closing my eyes to relax by the pool following our arrival, the area between my eyebrows was going crazy. I could feel and see with eyes closed the focusing and refocusing of acupoint *Tian Mu* like a camera lens adjusting at high speed. The movements were at an accelerated pace from what I was used to as my body processed a greater influx of spiritual energies.

The experience seemed to be equivalent to the illustrations of the Lovers card. Being in the sky above this sacred mountain I had intuitive spiritual experiences. Qigong practice had also made lucid dreaming more commonplace. Dream 35 teaches about the virtue of honoring spiritual diversity. We may each maintain a particular spiritual ideal but to be truly spiritual means honoring rather than condemning the different beliefs of others. Jesus Christ, the Holy Grail and the menstruating indigenous woman are truly a reflection of the same spiritual principle. The immortal golden vessel represents the Holy Grail as well as the holy blood within the feminine vessel of the human body. Each of us has this potential, as the dream of my own image shows. We just need to purify our bodies and cultivate our awareness of the divine to recognize that it comes from within.

Looking back, there were a number of synchronicities that facilitated my lucid dream experience. The flight was delayed a couple hours due to mechanical difficulties making my overflight of Uluru around sunset. I was seated on the right side of the aircraft and had a window seat, offering excellent views of Uluru during our flight. Then continued mechanical issues during the flight forced our plane to continue northbound to the city of Alice Springs rather than descend at the airport south of Uluru. There seemed to be a higher power at work, setting it up so that I would fly alongside Uluru with optimal views of this awesome megalith at sunset, a time when *yin* and *yang* merge to open a doorway to the Dreamtime.

The following day I walked around Uluru on foot and was honored to witness the profound healing that occurred when the newly elected Prime Minister of Australia Kevin Rudd gave a public apology to the Australian aboriginal people for wrongdoings of the past. I was impressed at the profound impact of the simple act of saying sorry as I watched crowds of people crying with tears of gratitude and relief. It was a great moment of healing for the country. The importance of venerating different cultural and spiritual beliefs shown in dream 35 had just been reinforced in physical life.

Dream 36: Lying down in my hotel room later the same day, I begin lucid dreaming right away. I see what looks like a real image of Uluru up close and clear in my mind. I note the individual features such as the curves and hollows of the mountain as well as the nearby vegetation. As I watch, I see the ground open up in front to form a rectangular passageway. Tall strong blue outlined beings with shining lights for heads walk towards the opening by the mountain. I see them disappear through the doorway and it closes after them.

The mythical Kunlun Mountain of China is the meeting point where the primordial brother and sister save the human race.[12] Kun Lun Mountain is a pillar between heaven and earth. It is the central axis where *yin* and *yang* balance. This metal gate is the mysterious pass where being and nonbeing interface to provide access to other dimensions of existence and the infinite Tao.

We see this also in the Lovers card mountain. The triangle shape of the mountain symbolizes cosmic unity between the Trinity of heaven, earth and humankind. Rising upwards from between the couple, the mountain ascends towards the angelic being above. The golden sun in the shape of the Ouroborus is once again a portal to other dimensions. As in Chinese myth, the primordial twin couple resurrect the human race by passing through this 'golden gate'.[12]

According to the Uluru National Park Visitor's Guide, the Australian Aborigines believe that the ancestors of the eternal Dreamtime continue to live within the Uluru mountain formation. Unaware of this at the time of dream 36 I would read about this upon returning home to the states a few weeks later. Similar ideas exist in other cultures as well. There are Norwegian stories of trolls changing into and being tall mountains. In Ireland, fairies are thought to live in fairy mounds with fairy rings as portals to other dimensions. The archangel Michael is likewise associated with different hillside settings in England.[13]

Tara Stone of Destiny at the apex of Tara Hill in Ireland. This sacred site is considered a spiritual womb and entrance to the Otherworld. It is also another sacred dwelling place of the Tuatha Dé Dannan, the Shining Ones.

Looking upon the angelic being with the fiery hair of this tarot card, I am reminded of my dream experience of these interdimensional angelic beings. Their shimmering heads of light appear like the halos we see around Christian saints, angels and other enlightened beings. I think these angelic beings are around us all the time yet seldom seen. They are, I believe, the enlightened immortal beings working etherically on our behalf. We can connect with these ancestral light beings through dreaming. They are a stepping down of the omnipotence of God energy in a form we can comprehend. Utilizing more of our brain capacity through Qigong Dreaming, we access esoteric wisdom from teachers of former ages.

All of creation passes through a symbolic doorway to return to the Tao. Some of the Taoist names for this gateway between being and nonbeing include golden portal, metal gate and mysterious pass. In *The Book of Balance and Harmony,* 13th century Taoist philosopher Li Daoqun called this door 'the heart of heaven'.[12] Here *yin* and *yang* merge alchemically to create a sphere of light.[48] The marriage of *yin* and *yang* occurs at the center of the heart in the middle *dan tian,* opening the golden gates of heaven for true healing.

Dream 37: I see images at different times in the middle of my chest including Jesus, the Egyptian divine couple Hathor with Horus and Osama Bin Laden.

One of my students gave me an Indian poster of the Monkey King opening his chest to reveal the divine Hindu couple Shiva and Parvati inside his heart. The Lovers card of the tarot likewise represents the sacred heart where *yin* and *yang* aspects unify as one within the middle *dan tian.* It was through intuitive awareness that I experienced Jesus Christ or Christ consciousness through my heart. The heart is the indwelling of the Holy Communion.

It was also validating to experience through dreaming the heart as the place where *yin* and *yang* soul reunite. The goddess and god Hathor and Horus symbolize this spiritual unification just like the woman and man in the Lovers card. Healing any perceived wrongdoings or limitations within ourselves, we align the masculine and feminine aspects of our soul. If there is an individual, such as Osama Bin Laden, who appears within our hearts, we have been given an opportunity to heal harmful, immoral, or evil associations with the personality of the individual. By clearing our negative perceptions, we heal our individual and collective regression into dualistic thinking. Negative emotional responses show which beliefs and thoughts are in need of healing. One can hold an individual who triggers anger, pity, grief, worry, etc. within the heart and through prayer like Qigong remove the filters of judgment until we see him or her as holy and perfect aspects of the divine.[49] At the soul level, we truly are all brethren and everything else is illusory. This is spiritual truth no matter how 'bad' the circumstance appears. Clearing our negative associations frees up the flow of energy in our Central Channel and allows Source to channel through. The situation or individual held within our heart then becomes immersed with central *qi* and can be transformed with unconditional love. There is no action I have found more powerful for transmuting the feelings of separation that divide us. Working with the one heart, one mind connection to the Tao, we help unlock the alchemical process within others as well as ourselves to ultimately bring higher states of awareness into this world. Using *ling* spiritual potency of the heart, we can become constructive agents for transcendental change and help consciousness evolve.

A 15th century alchemical Chinese drawing depicts a heart-shaped alchemical furnace heating and raising a spiritual adept towards immortality.[9] This image seems an appropriate demonstration for the alchemical transformations we can create when we work at the level of the heart. Working to free up central *qi* we can allow it to elevate us higher and higher. We begin to know that we, as humans, are vessels for the eternal and omnipotent.

> Some ancient Chinese alchemical pots are heart shaped. The rising steam of central qi from internal heating techniques gently opens the physical, emotional and spiritual centers (dan tian) of the body.

Dream 38: Christ appears and tells me he is the eternal presence within everything and everyone. He is replaced by Mary Magdalene, who explains how she represents the alchemical process of transformation and the Holy Grail. She is the means to liberate the self and cultivate the spiritual through the physical body.

Christian scholar Elaine Pagels, Ph.D. described two conflicting traditions of Christianity. Orthodox Christianity is represented by the teachings of the Apostle Peter, who, according to Mary Magdalene in the Pistis Sophia scripture, is he who 'hates the female race'. Peter's message was incorporated into the 4th century reproduction and editing of the New Testament. Any writings and teachings of Jesus that deviated from the doctrine established by the Council of Nicea in 326 CE became heretical and sanctioned for destruction.[42] Determined by majority vote of male church leaders, the agreed upon teachings downplayed spiritual feminine wisdom. The church of Mary Magdalene went underground, particularly during the Inquisition when fear of torture and death was widespread. However, Gnostic groups such as the Templars and Cathars held Mary Magdalene in high esteem and had contact with Eastern spiritual alchemical traditions. In the Gospel of Mary, a 2nd century text fortuitously found in a cave at Nag Hammadi in Egypt, Magdalene shares with the apostles direct teachings of Jesus Christ through visions and lectures following his resurrection.[42] *Apostle* is a Greek word for messenger. Mary is therefore the apostle to the apostles and demonstrates intuitive knowledge hidden from the others.[42]

The Gospel of Mary teaches that the heart is the way to relationship with the Divine.[42] Mary explains that visions come between the place of soul and Spirit. This is equivalent to Taoist and alchemical thought, which emphasizes spiritual knowledge based upon personal experience with the transcendental. Likewise, Lao Tzu's golden secret of all life is the space between zero and one. Zero is the infinite of Spirit and one is the unification of *yin* and *yang* as one soul. Metaphors for spiritual teachings are also found in the Bible. The serpent as a symbol for the Ouroborus spiral says to Eve, 'You won't really die'.[18] There is promise of spiritual immortality through the fruits of inner cultivation, though this spiritual wisdom has been clouded with judgments of blame and shame. Mary Magdalene is referred to in the New Testament as one from 'whom seven demons had gone out'. She demonstrates by this reference that she has purified the seven emotions of the *yin* body soul and is a spiritual adept. Seven is also the number of the Holy Spirit. The soul now purified channels down the Holy Spirit of divine light. This subtle reference in Luke 8:2 hints that Mary Magdalene knew the means of obtaining the immortal golden body. Looking at the quote from an Eastern symbolic perspective clarifies the symbolic meaning of this and other biblical references.

Christianity would benefit by embracing both Peter and Mary's teachings. Christianity, Judaism and Islam could all move back into *yin* and *yang* balance by teaching body-minded spiritual practices. Leaders of spiritual traditions could help elevate human consciousness by teaching inner cultivation techniques to cleanse the body and mind while helping individuals interpret divine guidance of dreams.

Chapter 19

The Chariot

Dream 39: I see the roots of a tree shift into a man climbing the trunk of a tree with a blue square on his t-shirt over his chest. The scene shifts into the image of the upper branches of the tree with stars dangling from their tips.
Dream 40: I see water flushed and spiraling down into a white toilet bowl. As I continue to watch a blue etheric square rises upwards from the toilet plumbing and into the air above.

The blue square upon the man's chest in Waite's Temperance card draws my attention as it reflects my own dreaming experience. I began dreaming of ascending blue squares to mark the completion of the *po* soul purification. The consciousness within my physical body had been awakened and begun to ascend towards the spiritual self. It is via the *hun* evolutionary soul, related to the element of wood, that the spiritual adept reaches the stars as metaphor for the upper world and heaven within.

In the Hindu Tantric system, the lowest chakra, *Muladhara,* literally means roots or root support.[50] In kundalini yoga, the tree is synonymous with the central axis of the universe. The coiled serpent as primary symbol of the kundalini force ascends from the earthly root base to the top of the tree. Here the mythical eagle Guarda carries the serpent into the air.[50] The union of serpent of the lower world and eagle of the upper world reflects the unity of *po* body soul with *hun* evolutionary soul. Rising into the air they return to the celestial treasure of the stars, associated with the middle *dan tian* in Chinese Medicine. Air is the element of the *Anahata,* or heart chakra in the kundalini yoga system. The journey of the united soul ultimately leads back to the heart. No wonder the ancient Qigong practitioners depict the wood energy, associated with the wind blowing through the leaves, as leading to and nourishing the fire of the heart.

Trees raise their leaves towards heaven while sinking their roots deep within the earth. They receive nourishment or life force energy from above and below. Likewise, the wood element in Chinese symbolism connects humanity with the upper and lower worlds. The wood element is, therefore, like the Central Channel and associated with central *qi* (think of those concentric tree rings). It is governed by the mythical dragon swirling amongst the clouds. The dragon is described in Chinese myth as the celestial vehicle carrying souls upon death to the Paradise of the Immortals.[12] Related with the middle *dan tian* of the body, the bridge between physical and spiritual worlds is governed by the archetype of the Chariot. Travelling in a chariot, the young man of this tarot card depicts the immortal body that can travel to the Dreamtime and access different dimensions of the universe.

In Chinese folklore, the Queen of the West rides a chariot led by flying horse or dragons. She wears tiger skins and represents the liberating agent of the metal element. She is also associated with the planet Venus. Venus is likewise both the evening star at sunset (death) as well as the morning star that precedes the dawn's rising of the solar light upon earth (rebirth).[17] To alchemists in ancient Greece, Egypt, India and Mesopotamia, the goddesses associated with the planet Venus had the alchemical power to kill off illusions and unify *yin* and *yang* polarity. Venus as a symbol of divine insight and intuition guides us in dreams through the alchemical works. She reflects the transcendental process that changes base metals into gold and humans into their higher selves.[17]

In this tarot card the virile young man is the charioteer. He is *yang* in gender and wears a crown encircled by green leaves representing wood. These traits show the strength of the *hun* soul and connection with spiritual nature. By contrast, he also wears silver metal armor and a crown topped by an eight-pointed star. Wearing the star of alchemy [17] he shows that his spiritual development results from the transformative power of bodywork. The opposing faced crescent moons upon the shoulders of the charioteer show the waning and waxing phases of the moon. The internal death to rebirth alchemical process of enlightenment is reflected by the cyclical phases of the moon in the night sky. Through the alchemical works complementary aspects of wood and metal element have been reunited together as one.

The Sphinx in Giza, Egypt gazes calmly to the east and is thought to have helped initiates ascend to the heavenly stars. The sphinxes that lead the chariot in this card are likewise heavenly messengers and symbols of the united soul. The black and white male headdress upon the sphinx's feminine lioness body shows the union of heavenly and earthly influences within. Like the black and white striped celestial tiger of Chinese Medicine they show the blending of *yin* and *yang* through internal metallurgy.

Dream 41: I see concentric circles up high in the night sky. I feel and see them vibrate, building energy until they finally explode forming the stars of the night sky. Looking down at my chest from where I watch from earth in the dream, I see the same image of concentric circles faintly illuminated upon my chest.

I would read the day following this dream that concentric circles represent the stars to the Australian Aborigines.[51] Star (or *sba* as it is termed in Egyptian) also means door. These star doors are pictured in Egyptian hieroglyphs along with the *ba,* or winged soul, a metaphysical concept similar to the *yang hun* soul of Asian thought. Dr. Charles Muses, mathematician and philosopher, explains the concept of going through these star doors as necessary in the Osirian transformation. Passing through star doors initiates a metamorphosis into the immortal body.[31]

Dream 41 seemed reminiscent of the big bang theory

regarding the creation and expansion of the universe following a giant explosion. It brings to my mind our original oneness prior to the creation of the universe. These star doors of our dreams may provide access to this primordial state that we are connected to in a dimension beyond time and space. Lao Tzu stated that through emptiness and inner awareness a doorway opens to the golden secret of all life. Working in a lucid dream state with the Ouroborus spiral symbol can open a celestial gateway, the golden gates of heaven, and be a way to return to the transcendental aspect of ourselves. Through Qigong Dreaming techniques we can move towards completing the metamorphosis of the physical to the immortal. As we physically transform we lighten up enjoying greater health and fulfillment. Remaining centered in our hearts we return to inner peace.

Double spiral showing the flow between the invisible and tangible in the ancient Greek city of Pergamon in modern day Turkey.

There is a free flowing and dynamic interchange between the mundane and the mystical. The immanent and transcendental aspects of reality are linked together like the infinity symbol. When we strengthen our brain's right hemisphere through Qigong, we connect with the mystical. Uniting with our celestial counterparts may begin in our minds but, as Lao Tzu taught, it also happens within our hearts. Obtaining one mind, one heart through the development of virtues (*de*) original nature is returned and destiny is fulfilled.[6]

The story of humanity's quest to reunite with heavenly origins is common in many traditions as well. In the Gnostic tradition, Sophia is the goddess of wisdom and daughter of the highest god.[52] Divine in nature, Sophia becomes separated from her masculine counterpart. Left out of balance, Sophia falls to earth and into the abyss of darkness. She abandons 'the way' of the heart and arrogantly seeks spiritual understanding through intellectual pursuits. She suffers great confusion and fear as a result. Gradually, however, the archetypes of *yin* and *yang*, dark and light, physical and spiritual, Holy Spirit and Christ, surround Sophia.[52] Christ ultimately liberates Sophia by awakening memories of divine union and bliss with God. Sophia personifies the soul of every person who is redeemed through self realization.[52]

Jesus as a religious figure provides inspiration. As a personal guide he helps the spiritual seeker achieve wisdom through inner awareness. Jesus as the *hun* evolutionary soul is also a part of each person. Jesus tells Thomas in John 14:5 to 6, 'I am the way, the truth, and the life…' We gain enlightenment and everlasting life awakening the avatar within. Cultivating inner awareness and development we remove spiritual obstacles that separate us from the savior within whether Jesus, Mohammad, Buddha, the Green Man, Odin, Dionysus or another spiritual embodied figurehead.

> *Dream 42: From within a stone-walled room I see a shaft opening to the outdoors. Looking through the upward angled square corridor I see a star on my right in the night sky.*
> *Dream 43: Doing a crystal bowel meditation at home, I see an etheric star ahead and to my right. Remembering dream 42, I wonder if it represents a missing piece of my soul. Sensing the right side of my chest, it feels hollow and empty. I invite the star as dream symbol into my middle* dan tian.

Anahata, the name for the heart chakra, literally means 'unstuck'.[36] Clearing out the old blockages of the past, there is an energetic void that needs to be filled. There is a part of us needing spiritual nourishment similar to the way our physical body needs food. Helping us go back to our origins, the image of the star in this case came through as a vitalizing energy. Translating the vibration behind the dream symbol, it became incorporated into my body. I could literally feel the energy of my middle *dan tian* grow, particularly on the right or etheric side of my middle *dan tian*. Spiritually reunited with some aspect of myself using this new Qigong Dreaming technique, I felt somehow more complete.

> Within the Great Pyramid of Giza in Egypt are shaft like openings to the stars.

Unifying the celestial and terrestrial aspects of the self through working with dream symbols is extremely healing. This may be why archetypal symbols have been engraved in rock and depicted in pictographs in ancient cultures around the world. Sacred images such as Reiki symbols and Nordic runes come from the universal and timeless dimension of the Dreamtime and are meant to be worked with. They come down from Source to guide and direct us in our lives. As visual codes, they also carry an energetic signature that we can access and convert within our bodies for greater physical, emotional, mental and spiritual healing. Working with sacred dream symbols has helped me heal my heart beyond what I thought possible. I have found it an extremely beneficial technique with students and clients as well. Helping reunite the splintered pieces of the soul (note that seven is the number of the Chariot card), we return to wholeness.

Dream 44: I see the Chariot card image before me as I practice Turtle Longevity Qigong in class. Lingering there for some time I ask if there is something I am forgetting that should be included in this book.

The above lucid dream example demonstrates another way of actively working with dream images to unlock their messages. Being in a receptive state as I moved with Qigong, I was open to receive additional intuitive information about the dream image. I will often feel, hear, or see additional impressions if I can keep my ego out of the way and not feel attached to what form the response comes in. In this case, the answer came through as a thought. I was not to forget about the basics and that *qi* is the unifying force that unites *yin* and *yang*, earth and heaven and *jing* essence with *shen* Spirit. Qi as the Chariot harmonizes the soul and interconnects us with all of creation and our divine origins.

In January 2005, the *New Scientist* reported that a US physicist at New York University, Glennys Farrar, had identified five ultra high energy cosmic rays originating from the direction of Ursa Major. What causes these cosmic gamma ray bursts remains unknown but they are hypothesized to be possibly linked to black hole activity. Taoist theory teaches that the five elements of Chinese Medicine are energies poured down from the Big Dipper. The different energies of wood, fire, earth, metal and water make up everything in the universe and within our own bodies. The energies from the Big Dipper imprint upon our bodies at conception and guide us forward towards fulfilling our individual destiny.[12] Holy Grail legends also depict the Big Dipper as the origin of important cosmic rays cascading down to Earth.[31] There are five empty spaces within the belt of the Chariot rider over a black background. Does this card depict the black holes as the source of these five specific cosmic rays? I cannot say. However, I have had the dream experience of being transported abruptly into what seemed to be a black hole. This experience leads me to believe that both the Taoists of ancient China and the alchemists of Europe were connected to wisdom of the universe through dreams – things that most of us are just beginning to understand scientifically. Dreams have furthered our understanding of the universe, significantly contributing to the sciences of physics, astronomy, chemistry, biology and psychology. Enlightening dreams often precede and guide scientific discovery.

Dream 45: The image of a white dove holding a white circle above me.
Dream 46: A white glowing cross upon the chest of a man. From the cross, the man creates a large white circular doorway.
Dream 47: Kwan Yin emerging from an illuminated vesica piscis.

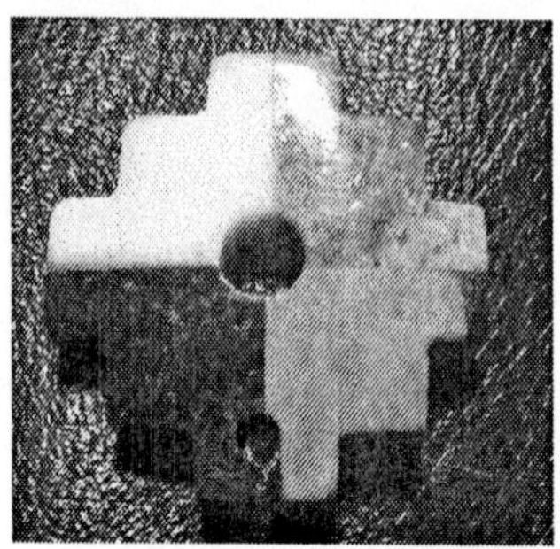

The Andean cross of South America shows the balance of the four directions around a central hole representing the infinite void of God.

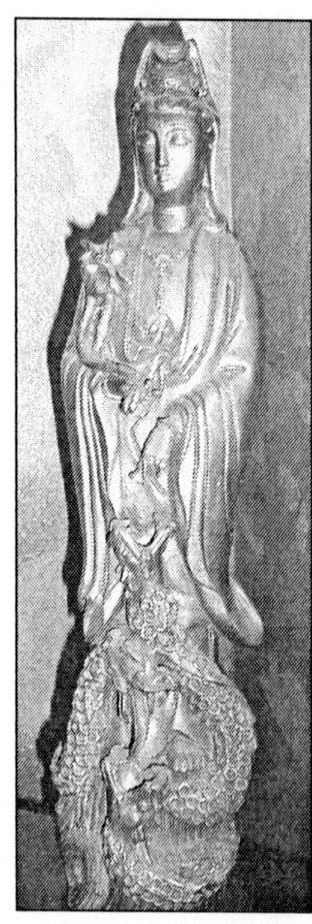

Kwan Yin is a Buddhist symbol of compassion. She purifies the sins of the world by dropping them into the mouths of three dragons rising from the ground below her feet.

The dove, cross and vesica piscis are additional versions of the Chariot and symbols to connect with higher dimensional energies. The descent of the Holy Spirit is often marked by the presence of a white dove in Christian scripture and religious artwork. The dove is also a symbol of love through connection with the Roman goddess Venus. Burning away destructive emotions upon the alchemical pot, only joy and love remain. Cleansed of illusion, we are open to receive divine grace from heaven. The cross is also a sacred symbol to many different traditions. Christ himself is often pictured with the center of the cross directly behind his chest. Like the man in dream 46 it is at the middle *dan tian* that the threshold to the circular Ouroborus is obtainable. The central point of the Andean cross, likewise, depicts a round hollow or emptiness representing the eternal and infinite of God. Through purity of heart we can find the transcendental Tao. An empty heart is a sacred heart. Dream 47 confirms this as a universal truth rather than a religious ideology. Here we find Kwan Yin, an enlightened being of Buddhism and symbol of feminine compassion, emerging from the fish-shaped vesica piscis symbol. Often connected to Jesus, this image is created when two opposing circles symbolizing *yin* and *yang* opposites overlap to create a unified and androgynous fish-like symbol of Christ consciousness. Spiritual energies of different traditions channel into our physical reality when we keep an open heart. Through this simple act we help manifest peace and goodwill for all sentient beings.

The vesica piscis is an ancient pre-Christian symbol on the cover of a sacred well at Glastonbury, England. Associated with the goddess Brigit it represents a sacred doorway between the spiritual/unconscious and material/conscious worlds. The red iron rich waters at this sacred site represent the sacred blood or central qi flowing up from the earth. This almond shaped symbol can also represents the vaginal CV-1 as a gateway to transcendental wisdom.

Chapter 20

The Hanged Man

Dream 48: I see a circle surrounding the midsection of a pole. The circle rises upwards on the pole to the top. At the apex it becomes the solar bindu *symbol. A man behind the pole picks up the encircled dot symbol and places it over his head. At this point the bindu symbol becomes a halo of golden light.*

Dream 48 combines the encircled pole on the emblem of the Chariot card with the golden halo of light around the Hanged Man. No wonder as both the Chariot and the Hanged Man cards are alchemically linked. They seemed at least to occur concurrently for me. The Chariot is the portal or bridge to the transcendental where the individual can rediscover his or her etheric or *yang* soul. The Hanged Man is a personification of the *hun* or evolutionary *yang* soul that we spiritually reunite with.

The upper *dan tian* in the center of the forehead is associated with the *yang* symbol of the sun. Halos of shining light around the head are also solar symbols of ancient Greece and Egypt.[13] The halo originated from the Eleusinian Mysteries of ancient Greece and represents the sacred act of god making. It was during a festival called Haloa that the savior wine god Dionysus was resurrected and deified.[53] In India, light around the head of an individual represents the

Jesus' head illuminated by the equidistant cross figured halo at the Hagia Sophia in Istanbul, Turkey.

'thousand petaled lotus of light' rising up from the seventh chakra of an enlightened being. A halo of light also became a symbol of divinity to Christian deities and saints.[54]

The wooden cross in the Hanged Man card is in a T or Tau shape. The tree is headless like the enlightened man hanging upside down. Through spiritual development one becomes in a sense headless. The consciousness becomes bodiless as an orb of light. The halo image in the Hanged Man and dream 48 depict this. John the Baptist, a key spiritual adept to the Gnostic Knights Templar, was said to have been beheaded after the goddess Salome, the kundalini personified, encircled him in the Dance of Seven Veils. Following seven rotations, representing the movement through the seven chakras, she took possession of his head.[29] To me, becoming headless represents the emptying of the ego personality. Then one can see oneself as the light within. Salome's possession of the mind represents the clearing of long held thoughts and beliefs that separate rather than unify us with God.

Dream 49: Series of dreams about crystal skulls including one followed by my computer in a bag and another one where the skull was on the ground surrounded by grass.

Crystals are translucent and clear silica stones. They are used in computers for their ability to store memory. Crystals are also sensitive to vibration and can be used to create radios as a means to pick up different signals. Crystal skulls have become a popular trend and are a symbol of oracular knowledge. Traditionally, they were believed to share the secrets of the afterlife.[2] Jesus was crucified on the Hill of Golgotha or 'Place of the Skull'.[29] This may highlight the association between spiritual adept and inner sight leading to wisdom. Associated with the spiritual qualities of the wood element in dream 49, the clarity of crystal gems reflects the divine light within.

The Norse God Odin acquired divine powers and the secrets of the runes following his Crucifixion. He was hung upside down like the Hanged Man. The Hanged Man is the twelfth card of the deck. The twelfth rune represents divination and magic. Both demonstrate the power to make the dead speak and enhance the ability to access ancient wisdom of the past.[55] This is what is esoterically referenced as the Akashic records. When our heads become crystal clear we are able to consciously tap into the wisdom of the collective unconscious through lucid dreaming. We bring the divine down to earth. The downward flow of transcendental wisdom is depicted by the upside down man in this card and the crystal skull on the ground in dream 49. The grounded skull reinforces the idea that matter can be spiritualized. Unlocking spiral energies within the earth facilitates our own enlightenment. The Hanged Man opens this acupoint through what looks like the yogic asana posture known as tree pose and the pose Australian Aborigines take while in the Bush. I have dreamed of a golden light emanating from CV-1 from a man in a similar position. Once again the importance of utilizing the body to free up the spiritual energies of the individual is emphasized in the tarot cards.

The green dragon is the celestial representation of the East and rebirth of life at spring.

The connection between a spiritual adept and the wood element is pervasive in different myths around the world. Odin hung upside down upon the World Tree for nine days and nights. He, like the crucified Jesus, was pierced by a spear in the right side of his ribcage. Both saviors bled from the anatomical area of the liver and gall bladder, the two organs associated with the wood element. Gautama Buddha was born from the right side of his mother Maya and became enlightened while meditating under the Bodhi tree. The Egyptian god Osiris was entombed within a tree and later resurrected by his sister Isis in a spiritual rebirth. The Mayan savior Quetzalcoatl is described as a green serpent (a double wood connection) deity. Taoist, European and Middle Eastern alchemists associated trees with the elixir of life. It is also the magical trees of Greek, Chinese, Norse and Celtic myths that bear the apples of immortality.[13]

:Cernunnos is a pagan Celtic god of nature from Western Europe. In some images he holds a serpent (1) and a spiraling circular Ouroborus symbol (0).

Dream 50: Awake one morning I hear, 'Dragon bodies are the basis of Christ, Christ consciousness.'
Dream 51: 'Essenes used alchemical fire to transform the body and achieve immortality.'
Dream 52: In a walk I observe a large etheric flower of life merkaba above me. Later I experience the merkaba around my body as ascending and descending spirals of energy.

I thought I recalled reading something about dragon bodies in Mark Amaru Pinkham's *The Return of the Serpents of Wisdom* and so I pulled it out following dream 50. Pinkham described the immortal dragon body as an etheric vehicle of light created through physical purification and meditative techniques employed by Taoist sages. The dragon body, he continues, is also the immortal fetus due to the cultivation and transformation of *jing* essence in the lower abdomen, the area

Early woodcut of the liver from ancient China shows an upside down lotus flower. Author dreamed of herself wearing an upside down yellow flower dress on the Celtic festival of Beltaine.

The resurrected vegetative wine god of the Greek Mysteries Dionysus. Dionysus was associated with physical healing, prophesy and spiritual illumination through the letting go of the ego mind.

where the pregnant carry their young. Tiger (*yin* soul) and dragon (*yang* soul) ultimately unite, giving the spiritual adept the ability to travel to the heavenly Realm of the Immortals.[5]

Pinkham also spoke of the ancient Hebrew community called the Essenes, who revived the ancient mystical teachings of earlier prophets and the Levites. Based upon mystical Judaic knowledge passed by Moses and Abraham, and influenced by teachings from Asia, the goal of these peaceful people was to reawaken intuitive knowledge of the heart. According to the Essenes, Moses saw the forces of nature and human consciousness as angels.[56] Communion with these angelic forces was how individuals connected with God, the supreme and eternal One Law governing everything in the universe. Harmonizing with these forces and spending time in nature helped the Essenes evolve in body and spirit.[56] Communion continues today through Qigong, a nature based practice rooted in the ancient traditions of China.

Essene teachings later included meditations and the study of the Kabala, the Torah and the Book of Enoch.[5] Individuals were believed to travel to the highest heavens in their *merkaba,* the Jewish title for the dragon body. *Mer* means light, with *ka* and *ba* (Egyptian terms for lower and upper dragon bodies) the *yin* and *yang* soul respectively. The merkaba is an interdimensional vehicle also described in Buddhist texts as counter rotating fields of light that can carry consciousness to higher dimensions.[31]

Jesus' spiritual education appears to have incorporated Essene teachings while he was in Egypt and later in Palestine.[5] He is later believed to have taught the esoteric teachings of the Essenes, using the Kabala of the human body to awaken the *shekinah* or kundalini power.[5] Jesus passed his knowledge of alchemy to the disciples helping them likewise become Christed: a title for one who becomes awakened to their authenticity and is enlightened. Jesus taught that the divinity of God exists within the hearts of everyone. The sacred heart is the indwelling of 'the kingdom of heaven'.[5] Cautioning others to act responsibly by directing the serpent power through the opened heart, Jesus advised 'Be wise as serpents and harmless as doves'.

Dream 53: I am driving on the left side of the road. I need to move to the right and I worry about oncoming traffic trying to change lanes. Looking in the rear view mirror, I see that there is no one blocking my path and I can change lanes without worry.
Dream 54: I see Mother Mary with a young golden Jesus upon her lap. He is on the right side and pointing towards the right and the direction of the East.

Dream 53 showed me I was ready and needed to make another move to the right. I just had to figure out what the right side represented in this case. Dream 54 came along a few days later with additional promptings and some clarification. Here Jesus as the golden child, the immortal golden embryo symbol, points to the East. I recognized that I spiritually needed to move

Jesus in Mother Mary's lap in the Chora Church Istanbul, Turkey. The lower dan tian is where we can align personal will with divine will in the journey to authentic living.

more to the right. I was being told to develop the *yang* aspect of the wood element or *hun* evolutionary soul. How I was to do this, I was not sure. I had nothing to worry about as the answer came soon thereafter.

> *Dream 55: Tired one night after work, I sit down on the couch and close my eyes. Immediately, I see a woman in my mind's eye looking at me. She moves her right hand in a counterclockwise direction in the air and creates a circular Ouroborus that remains visible. The woman then enlarges the Ouroborus - until it is about human size. She walks through the circle to another dimension and I can no longer see her. A few seconds later she peaks her head out again to look at me.*

Needless to say, I was a little – okay maybe a lot – taken aback by what I had just witnessed. This most recent dream experience left little room for misinterpretation, the nonverbal communications reminding me of a Lassie rerun. I was to consciously create the Ouroborus shape I had been using to clear away and transform nightmares and low vibrational energies but this time energetically walk through it with my dream self. A little nervous, I waited until late that night until the kids and my husband were asleep. I lay next to my unknowing husband Karl. Somehow, his presence gave me comfort and assurance as I embarked on this new Qigong Dreaming assignment. I proceeded to create and expand the Ouroborus as I had been shown and sent my etheric dreaming self through the symbol. I was acting on faith and trust but I knew from previous experience that my dreams had always been my highest form of spiritual guidance and could be trusted. The other side felt to me like empty space, a void. I had the impression I was to remain on the other side of this looking glass for three days before returning. I noted afterwards that this occurred about 10 pm on March 17, about three days before the spring equinox. The equinoxes, like dawn and dusk, represent a natural balance of *yin* and *yang* energies and are, as such, potent times for intuitive dreaming as the veils of illusion are thinner.

Walking my son to school the next morning, we passed the Lutheran Church where he had attended preschool years earlier and where I was taking yoga once a week. Looking upon the building-sized cross on the property, I had an inexplicable emotional response – something beyond anything I had previously experienced, though I routinely pass by and admire the cross regularly. I pondered my unusual reaction and wondered if working with the Ouroborus symbol was similar to the Crucifixion. In accordance with the spring energies of the season, I followed Jesus' example and consciously let go of any and all angers, resentments and egoist thoughts and beliefs. I focused my intention on clearing my liver and gall bladder wood energy of outdated issues of judgment and attachment and sent all the items into the O shaped Ouroborus to be purified. I handed over my issues, being able to let go of them by forgiving myself, the situation and anyone I might have perceived in the past as causing me harm. In a sense, I was putting my old items upon the cross on the other side of the spiraling dragon circle. I was once again sacrificing or shedding my old self so I could be reborn.

Dream 56: I am playfully flying up and down between the earth and sky. From way up high, I begin to freefall. Falling with great speed, my body horizontal with arms outstretched and face upwards, I calmly realize that I am going to die but do not resist. In an instant my body transforms into a bird and I fly upside down thinking I need to tell my husband to look for me as a bird when I die.

In Norse mythology, Odin hung upside down on the World Tree called Yggdasil. Joseph Campbell described Odin's actions as self sacrifice to the greater consciousness within.[46] Metaphorically we could say the same thing about anyone willing and able to let

Human headed birds at Rumi's museum in Konya, Turkey may depict the Chinese hun evolutionary soul as well as the Egyptian ba soul.

go of fears and attachments. In dream 56 I am travelling between the earth and the sky, between the worlds of the immanent and the transcendental. I calmly face and overcome fears of my own physical mortality showing confidence and faith in the outcome. Greeting death without fear, I seem to have passed another initiation. My transformation into a symbol of spiritual transcendence shows spiritual progress.

The upside down orientation seems interesting to me. Could this represent the mirror reflection of the spiritual world within matter? Perhaps my bird-like characteristics represent the immortal body consciousness living outside and beyond physical constraints.

Dream 57: I am on the top of the Tau cross with Jesus. Our arms interlock in the shape of the infinity sign. Jesus puts a golden ring on my left index finger. Looking around us, I don't see anyone else. I wish more people were up here with us to share this experience.

Dream 58: I see the face of a man in a tree trunk that seems somewhere in Ireland. He is part of the tree and has leaves around his face. The pagan image of the Green Man asks me to help clear the energy lines of past trauma from his ancient sacred sites.

I include the above dreams for a couple of reasons. One is to highlight the importance of rising above our challenges in life. Being above the crosses we bear, we have an opportunity to rise above and transcend the energy. When we feel overwhelmed, we can connect with our greater self aligning the internal treasures within the Central Channel. Working with sacred dream symbols, we can also offer up and let go of the things that burden our hearts to a power higher than our limited personality and ego mind. Using the Ouroborus with intention had a beneficial effect as dream 57 shows. I have risen above my personal cross and reunited with Jesus, a metaphor for the East and a symbol of my purified *yang* soul. Here was my needed link to the eternal and infinite as shown by the symbol of our arms united.

Dreams guide us individually but they are also meant to be shared, thus the importance of dream groups. Enlightenment is, after all, not an individual journey; it is a collective assignment. We are each unique beings with our own authentic creative talents and our individual purpose but we are all here to wake up and recognize our higher selves. As we awaken to the unity consciousness permeating all of life, the delineation of self and other becomes blurred and more dreamlike. We may be like the trees, individual in one sense with our own trunk, roots and branches but, like a forest we also serve a collective function. We feel and know ourselves as the waves, a tiger, the moon, the earth, etc. when we do Qigong. Not only does it feel good. The practice cannot but expand our concept of a bigger self.

Through our practice, we cultivate benevolence, the virtue of the wood element. Kindness, compassion and goodwill for all is the basis of healthy community just as the Bible and other spiritual texts teach. We might physically do Qigong from one specific location yet with our minds we may journey anywhere in the universe. Through spontaneous Qigong we enter the Dreamtime, a dimension where time and space are irrelevant concepts. The Qigong student will often be guided towards planetary healing as I was in dream 58. No matter what our unique purpose, when we follow our destiny, the joy that results cannot but benefit others. Finally, we can dedicate our actions to help others. Think globally and act locally with your practice of Qigong as both are intricately linked.

Chapter 21

Strength

Dream 59: I see a close up view of my head. I open my mouth and pull on the tip of my tongue and watch as a black fluid cascades out of my mouth and down to the floor.

Dream 60: The image of a man coughing up junk out of his mouth.

The Hindu goddess Kali is often pictured with an elongated blood red tongue. She represents the Black stage of alchemy.

The first dream image reminds me of the female Hindu goddess Kali, often pictured with a skull necklace around her neck, a machete-like knife in her hand and an elongated and blood red tongue sticking out of her mouth. Kali is the black goddess of death and through symbolic killing removes all impurities of body and mind, figuratively depicted as junk in dream 60. Kali eliminates the illusion of separation from Spirit with her metal knife. She is the personification of the kundalini's purification process and the black stage of the alchemical works. As the tongue marks the end of the Conception Vessel, Kali's outstretched tongue also represent the downward flow of the microcosmic orbit, seen as black flowing liquid in dream 59 – the root of all *yin* energy in the body.

The kundalini is sometimes depicted by a goddess riding a lion and holding a drum.[32] In Waite's Strength card, the woman in white is like the Queen of the West, white being the color of metal. The Queen of the West was known to be fond of whistling. Likewise, the woman in the Strength card is shown with her hands around the lion's opened mouth, emphasizing the importance of the expression of voice in energetic healing. In the progression of spontaneous Qigong practice, the healing work moves from clearing out the lower body to removing stuck energy from the upper body. When this occurs crying, shouting, coughing, sighing, singing and laughter may all arise spontaneously as unexpressed emotions to be cleared. Allowing a spontaneous exhalation of the breath is also a method of releasing toxicity from the body. Just allow the throat to contract and release naturally if this happens during Spiral Qigong.

The white goddess figure of the Strength card is the personified kundalini. She is equal in her actions to the Hindu goddess Parvati who, through closing off the throat of her partner Shiva, helped destroy the poisons of the world. We see the woman's hands upon either side of the lion's mouth. Through her hand position she guides the cyclical flow of the microcosmic orbit downward and facilitates the transition between Governing and Conception Vessels. The lion himself is a spiritual adept who from the outstretched tongue position is purging his emotions and toxins through sacred sound. His tail tucked underneath closes off CV-1 allowing spontaneous contractions to vitalize the Central Channel with central *qi* from within the earth. Like a primed pump, this effort activates his voice as a powerful tool for clearing.

Red and white colored pictograph of She Who Watches in the Columbia Gorge, USA has large owl like eyes and swollen protruding tongue to emphasize her deathlike appearance. Her image sits up high and is a symbol of protection.

The lion is shown with a spiraling golden mane. Like the Hanged Man he is a symbol of the sun and the divine Presence in physical form. Both he and the woman are gigantic compared to their surroundings. The lion's head is above the mountain. He is connected with the transcendental and through his efforts has become a pure channel for the vibrations of God.

Dream 61: During Qigong, I feel the energy of green vegetation coming down from the heavens and through my Central Channel. I feel the energy spiral down around me in a clockwise direction.
Dream 62: I see a belt moving in a circle in a clockwise direction.

Garlands encircle the head and waist of the female figure. The previous, nearly leafless, wooden cross of the Hanged Man is now lush and blooming. Creative spiritual energies flow unrestricted for health, joy and spiritual bliss. They flow downward in a clockwise spiral from the heavens connecting with the earth behind the white dress of the woman. The landscape of the card is also lush and fertile. The Qigong student, by becoming a clear channel for life force energy, spreads order and harmony throughout the world.

The *Dai Mai,* also known as the Belt or Girdle Channel, encircles the waist and regulates the flow of the other energy channels of the body that flow in a vertical orientation. The Girdle Channel is sometimes associated with past karma and inherited family issues. As the energy of the Belt Channel clears, particularly through shouting, the sound of the wood channel, the energy begins to feel and appear healthier. A harmonious Belt Channel with healthy wood energy is shown in the Strength card by the green leaves and healthy red blossoms of the garland encircling the waist of the woman. Like springtime, the season of wood, the healthy foliage reflects renewal and rebirth.

Dream 63: I open my mouth and out comes a lion's roar.
Dream 64: I wake hearing the words, 'The mouth is the channel for the voice of God'.

Dream 65: 'The Muse, the one who channels in the raw power of the sun'.

In the Old Testament, Job had three beautiful daughters whose names can be translated as Dove, Cinnamon and Horn of Kohl.[31] Job gave each of his daughters a golden box as their inheritance. Within the boxes were golden shimmering bands that sparkled like rays of the sun. Job told his daughters that these sashes were gifts from God and would help them sustain life and lead them to a life in heaven.[31] When the sisters put the sashes around their waists, they received new hearts and could sing and understand the language of the angels. Their angelic communications revealed insight into the workings of heaven.[31]

The names of the three daughters represent different alchemical stages of transformation: kohl black for *Negrido,* dove white for *Albedo* and cinnamon red for *Rubedo*. These three colors are also symbolic of the triple goddess and the three *dan tian*. Black is the color of *yin* and the lower dan tian, white is the color of *yang* and of the upper dan tian and red the color of the central *qi* unifying the two extremes.

The daughters in the story inherited the golden sashes from God. The sashes remind me of deities such as Aphrodite who wore magical girdles around their waists to restore eternal youth and beauty. By putting on golden sashes, Job's daughters received gifts of longevity and eternal life. Clearing past karma helped them renew their hearts and speak the language of the gods, the energetic *qi* vibration of sound.

The Greek sun god Apollo was associated with the golden mane of the lion and the music of the muses. As the god of healing and prophesy, he was patron of oracular sites in modern day Turkey and Greece. Apollo was also the god of music and is often pictured carrying his musical instrument, the lyre. Perhaps Apollo's healing abilities are in fact attributed to the musical scale produced by the seven-stringed instrument he carries. Like the golden sun, Apollo has no shadow and is a metaphor for the eternal and divine spark of the soul. Playing his lyre, Apollo channels the primordial sounds of God.

The Buddha roared like a lion at his birth to depict his innate connection with the transcendent. His roar was a proclamation of his Buddha nature to the universe. We are all spiritual adepts discovering our innate divinity. Upon clearing physical, emotional and mental toxins through movement, intension, sound and breath work, the Central Channel becomes a hollow musical instrument. It is like the Australian aboriginal didgeridoo. Sufficiently purified, the voice becomes a direct link to 'the raw power of the sun'. Like the angelic being blowing the trumpet in the clouds of the Judgment card, spontaneous sound is the vibration preceding matter and the musical impulse that enlivens the spiritual within the physical.

Statue of Apollo the Greek god of the sun and music with his lyre. He represents the enlightened mind overcoming the destructive baser tendencies of human nature.

The lion is an animal of power to the Chinese. They can be found depicted in statue form with their tongues sticking out like the lion in the Strength card. Lions protect the living and the dead and magically call forth the rains.[57] This ability to bring the rains links them with the Chinese shamans who restored harmony and balance to the land through *ling* spiritual potency. Ritual dance and sound became the means for mystical union with the Tao. Spontaneous movement and verbal communications continue to be a powerful way to restore harmony to our physical existence.

Dreams 63 to 65 show the power and strength of using the

The didgeridoo is a wind instrument of the Aboriginal people of Northern Australian. The straight termite hollowed tree is similar to depictions of the Central Channel.

Lions are often pictured with spiraling coils in their manes in Turkey and Egypt. It is also common to find Buddha represented with spirals in his hair.

voice. At the time of these dreams, I was using breath work to initiate lucid dreaming. I also used the breath with intention to help clear the energy channels of clients during acupuncture, shiatsu massage and Reiki sessions. Using spontaneous sound with Qigong led to very powerful healing experiences for myself and students. However, the above dreams seemed to be prompting me forward to further understand how to work with sacred sound.

Dream 66: I am in a circle of people with my friend Denise. She states to the group, 'I believe in the infinite power of the universe.' I tell her I agree, then remember to ask if she knows of any classes I should take.

My friend Denise believes, as I do, in the abundance of the universe – that there is no end to what we can attract into our lives through the power of positive thoughts, beliefs and intentions (once subconscious resistances are resolved). I wondered following dream 66 if perhaps Denise might know of some interesting sound healing classes. I emailed her the following day, sharing my dream and my wish to learn more about working with sound. She replied with two options that she knew of, one of which was the upcoming annual Sound Healing Intensive by

Jonathan Goldman.

A friend of mine had kindly given me one of Goldman's CDs, entitled *Chakra Chants*, several months earlier. I had immediately liked it and was using it in my Spiral Qigong classes and in personal meditations. Once, following a fifth chakra chant to spontaneous movement and a toning exercise, I looked down and saw a glowing light in my heart. I had also taken the CD to Egypt with me and had deep mystical experiences while listening to it. I knew when I saw the Sound Healing Intensive that this was the class I was meant to attend. I promptly registered as I was due to leave for Peru the following week. The timing was most fortunate as I returned a few weeks later to find the class had filled.

Einstein taught that all physical matter is inherently energy and depicted this concept with the formula $E=mc^2$. Everything solid that we touch, such as this book you are reading, is made of atoms constantly in motion. Everything, including electrons, cells, organs, planets and galaxies, vibrates and in so doing creates sound. We as humans can only hear a narrow range of this electromagnetic scale with our ears yet there is music going on within and around us all the time.

Goldman explained during the Sound Healing Intensive that we each reflect a state of vibration. Each organ, bone, tissue and cell has a rhythm and fluidity. Together the body as a whole creates the 'Symphony of Self'. If a part of the body is off key or out of synch, disease can occur. Through sound as a healing modality, however, harmony can be restored for health and well being.

Sound is one aspect of *qi* or life force energy. In Qigong and Oriental Medicine, each organ has its own function and sound. Toning and movement exercises help clear and balance the elements that together make up the whole body. In Shiatsu Japanese bodywork, we were trained to feel through touch the vibrational state of the different energy meridians. With practice, one can learn to sense how the wood channels feel different from the fire channels, for example. I discovered that healthy and stressed energy channels feel qualitatively different. I had noted in my work that feelings, dream images and sounds could shift the energy of the whole channel of a client, sometimes instantly. This is also the case with Qigong, where spontaneous sounds coming through the mouth quickly shift and rebalance the body energetics. My experience has shown me that what Goldman taught is correct; we have the potential, working with energy vibration and sound, to shift our frequencies to higher levels of vibration for ascension and the evolution of consciousness.

> *Dream 67: Following a laughter therapy session at the Sound Healing Intensive I lie down and close my eyes. I soon see and feel a sacred temple in my mind's eye. I watch the triangular sides of the pyramid shape of the temple for several seconds before realizing the temple is within my own heart.*

The prophet Mohammad said, 'Consult your heart and hear the secret ordinance of God, discovered by the inward knowledge of the heart which is faith and divinity',[31] Having childlike faith and a sense of our own divinity, like the Fool, we act authentically. Our actions come from the heart instead of unhealthy filters like judging thoughts and residue from emotional trauma. Science shows that the heart has its own neural cells which are independent of the brain. Research into the innate intelligence of this organ is beginning to show how electromagnetic *qi* waves influence body systems and the brain.[32] The link between happiness and spiritual illumination is becoming clearer and clearer. Dream 67 shows that we can tune into Spirit by living in joy and that laughter can be a healing influence in our lives. It is the authentic expression of an awakened heart.

The electromagnetic field of the heart is 100 to 1000 times greater than that of the brain according to Jonathan Goldman. Of the whole body, the heart seems to send out the strongest electromagnetic impulse. The heartbeat is created from specialized heart tissue called the sino auricular node. It is independent of the brain and other body systems. Perhaps this heartbeat vibration is why Chinese sages consider the heart to be the Emperor of the body. When blood pumps through the heart, it is said to become red and filled with Spirit according to Chinese Medicine.[26] We know from research that the hemoglobin of blood cells exposed to different sound velocities changes shape.[58] The heartbeat may entrain the blood to vibrate at its same frequency. We are just beginning to understand that sound may nourish the cells of the body in subtle ways.

The heart is a potent place to focus intention. People often bring their hands together at heart level in a state of prayer. Goldman stressed that sound + intention = manifestation. My experience has been that heart + intention = manifestation, which is really saying the same thing, as the heart is the sacred chamber for generating sacred sound. We are always involved in the act of creation; it's just a matter of whether we do so consciously or not. Miracles are a matter of the heart. The purer one's heart song, the clearer I believe the electromagnetic message to the universe and the resulting physical manifestation response.

Goldman also gave me a new perspective on how sound can contribute to healing. Music has always been incorporated in healing and spiritual practices of our ancestors whatever lineage or tradition we come from. The Schumann Resonance is the electromagnetic field of the earth and has an average frequency of 7.83 Hertz. This frequency for the brain is the low range of alpha state associated with daydreaming and meditation. It is also the high range of theta brain frequency, associated with shamanic healing. According to Goldman, children's brains often function at the theta state. This is the state where wounding can occur. We each need to return to this theta state for healing the wounds and traumas of childhood. Spiral Qigong as a moving meditation is, I believe, a way to return to the theta state for healing subconscious wounds. Perhaps the central *qi* if heard would be the same frequency as the Schumann Resonance.

> *Dream 68: I see an image of sunlight reflecting off water and know that I am to work with the vibrations of dream symbols and other images. My path is to continue with dream healing and help train others.*

Following a didgeridoo healing session at the Sound Healing Intensive, I sat outdoors in a little garden enclave. It felt like something within me was unfolding in the right side of my chest and was being nourished and enlivened by the earlier sounds of my session. With increased awareness, I used my right hand to connect with the rocks, flies, birds and trees around me. I could hear their independent and collective song through my palm. I felt and knew that each animal, plant and mineral plays an important part in the overall musical symphony of life. This often-hidden reality of sound and vibration is a key to bridge the immanent world we live in with the transcendent. Sound is the angelic language and intermediary in the stepping down of Source energy. Synchronizing with nature's harmonics helps us return to our original bliss.

That night I awoke around 3 am unable to sleep. Lying relaxed on my side in bed, I let my right arm spontaneously move. I was experiencing lucid visual dreams and letting my heart move me. Connecting in with the dream images, I could hear their sound and translate their energetic signature. I seemed to be accessing and absorbing the vibrational blueprint behind the images and experiencing them as divine codes of healing. I felt an energetic response in my right chest each time I heard the symbols' song. My arm came to rest when I saw a final image – that of Duamutef, the jackal-headed god representing the East, on an embalming jar of ancient Egypt. I watched as the image entering into my middle *dan tian.* It became smaller and smaller until it completely disappeared deep within my chest. Then our burst a field of golden light from the darkness that filled the right aspect of my chest with an emanating glowing warmth. Something profound had taken place and my chest had never felt so good. I was most appreciative for this latest gift of healing and had a clearer understanding of my prior dream. I was to work with sacred dream images and translate their energetic signals through Qigong Dreaming.

Canopic jar of jackal headed god Duamutef represents the direction of the East to the ancient Egyptians.

The stepping down process of divine energy corresponds to the Hindu chakra system: Source energy at the seventh chakra comes down a step as sacred dream images to the sixth chakra at the forehead. Sight is then translated into sound vibration at the fifth chakra in the neck so it can next be integrated at the soul level at the heart in the fourth chakra. As I was told, the timing was right and my Central Channel was sufficiently clear to allow me to be an energetic transducer. I finally understood the meaning behind the famous Zen meditation koan: 'What is the sound of one hand clapping?' When we begin to hear the sound beneath the surface of what we perceive as reality, we can unlock the secrets of creation.

Chapter 22

The World

Dream 69: Going off to sleep, I ponder, 'What is God?' I see a circle of clouds with empty space in the middle.

Sufism is a mystical branch of the Muslim faith. The Sufi Hallaj said 'An'l Haqq' which translated means 'I am the Truth', 'I am the Reality', or 'I am God.'[59] The 13th century Sufi poet and spiritual master Mawlana Jalaladdeen Rumi created beautiful poetry while spiraling his body in a counterclockwise circle in what became the ecstatic spiritual practice called the whirling dervish. Whirling dervishes continue to be a technique for some sects of the Sufi tradition. It is an alchemical means to harmonize body, mind and heart, the three internal treasures in Chinese Medicine, with all life. Right palm held up high towards the sky, left palm held down towards the earth, the whirling dervishes are a means to unify heaven with earth and reinforce 'the Way' to achieve union with God. Guiding heavenly energies into the earth through intention it is another means to liberate the transcendental power of central *qi* as well as oneself.

Whirling dervish performers channel heavenly energies to earth focusing on their downward turned left hand as they spiral around in a counterclockwise direction.

In my travels through Turkey with author and goddess historian Karen Tate, I saw a whirling dervish performance. Watching this body-oriented spiritual practice I was immediately aware of the similarities to Qigong. The movements were a beautiful expression of love and joy. Later I visited the tomb of Rumi at the Mevlana museum in the Turkish city of Konya. Exploring the artwork of this original lodge of the Sufi Mevlevi whirling dervishes, I noted Chinese-looking pictures of people and dragons upon the walls. My Turkish tour guide confirmed the influence of ancient Chinese culture on the nomadic Turkish ancestors over the centuries.

Double headed green dragon picture at the Rumi Museum in Konya, Turkey.

Rumi observed in poem #1288, 'Hallaj said what he said and went to the Origin through the hole in the scaffold'.[59] The hole in this poem is the inner space of the Ouroborus. The Origin as our timeless beginnings would be comparable to the Tao. It is the eternal God also known as Allah to Muslims. Dragons associated with the Tao are pictured in Chinese art as clouds in the sky. When terrestrial based they are the greenness of the plant world. In dream 69 the clouds themselves form the Ouroborus shape and the way to heaven. In the World card the vegetative ring within a circle of clouds depicts the dragon symbol of transcendence in physical form. Both show spiritual symbolism of the East direction where the sun rises to remove darkness and illuminate the land. Replacing ignorance with wisdom is the message of Waite's tarot illustrations (recollect that he belonged to the Hermetic Order of the Golden Dawn) and Lao Tzu's *Tao De Jing*. But don't take my word on it. You can heal your wounds and find illumination through your own dreams. Qigong is a tool that can facilitate the process.

The Celtic Tree of Life unites heaven above with earth below. The rings of a tree also make the wood element a sensible representative of central qi in nature. The face in the picture is an image of the Green Man.

In the Waite World card, we specifically see a young woman whirling or dancing in the air encircled by a purple spiraled cloth. She depicts union with God in human form. Replace the woman with the cross and you have a symbol of the Resurrection of Christ found in many Catholic Churches. The central *qi* has raised the individual above the physical world. The purple color, associated with the crown chakra, shows the rise of kundalini energies to the top of the head. The spiritual journey is complete when oneness consciousness has thus been obtained.

The Chinese character for the *yang* evolutionary soul, called *hun,* is a depiction of clouds with an upright ghost. Upon death, the *yang* soul exits through the top of the head at acupoint GV-20 to ascend to the Big Dipper.[12] Having united with the *yin* soul called *po,* the individual from a Taoist perspective is ensured eternal life among the Immortals. Completing the Great Work of alchemy, he or she has through purification united soul with Spirit.

The movement of the Tao is represented energetically around the body as the microcosmic orbit. Energies ascend up the spine along the Governing Vessel and descend along the front midline of the body along the Conception Vessel. A continuous movement of transcendental spiral energy can be seen around the vegetation encircling the whirling figure. The World Card is number 21 or 2:1. When dual opposites of *yin* feminine and *yang* masculine merge as one, heaven on earth is obtained and an

Green jade is a precious stone commonly worn by women in China at heart level to nourish the blood. Known as the jade pi disc the hole in the center represents the pole star and the Absolute Oneness of the Tao. The object was believed in ancient times to guide the soul of the deceased to heaven.

individual has returned to the Tao.

In the World card, the Conception Vessel and Governing Vessel are united or tied together with red ribbon at two locations. The lower position of the kundalini awakening is the perineum floor of the body between the legs. This important opening, referred to as acupoint CV-1, is an important gateway for connecting with central *qi* for healing and wellness. The upper position is where the tongue touches the upper palate within the mouth. Clearing the voice and throat through sound also facilitates connection with Source. Uniting these two points in Qigong we complete the energetic circuit and blend these dual energies together as one.

This golden colored dragon is found amongst spiral shaped clouds in the sky and represent the Taoist concept of the immortal dragon body.

Dream 70: I see a circular ring with a garden of trees within the center.
Dream 71: The image of the earth appears with a white cross within the planet's interior core.

In medieval European artwork, angels are often depicted among the clouds in the circular mandala shape seen in the World card. These angelic cherubim represent the four elements and are symbolized by the lion, bull, serpent and eagle that guard the gates of Eden.[60] Dragons are, likewise, historically a conglomerate of different animals. In a dragon image from 206 BCE found in Inan, China, the lion's head, serpent scales, eagle's wings and bull horn are all apparent.[61] Other high ranking angels are the Seraphim. The word Seraphim translates as fiery serpents. These angels are responsible for awakening the divine wisdom within individuals.[5] Perhaps they are our higher selves guiding us through the Dreamtime and mediating our spiritual evolution or union with the Divine.

In the World card, the balance of the elements is depicted by the cardinal astrological signs of Leo the lion, Aquarius the angel, Taurus the bull and Scorpio the eagle. Yet, it is the fire sign of Leo that is the largest and looks directly at the viewer in this tarot card. We hold within us the fire of the Central sun. During our

The lion, the eagle, the bull and the young maiden represent the four signs around the winged Egyptian goddess of truth Maat holding a spiraling pole topped by the Ankh symbol of eternal life. They would later represent the four Evangelists of Christianity.

time in this world spiritual development is of most importance to humanity.

From a Chinese perspective, the four outside figures demonstrate the balance of water, metal, fire and wood leading to the stable element of earth or the world. Depicted as golden yellow, like the hair of the maiden in the World card, the fifth element is the central stability of individual wholeness. Having acquired psychological wholeness, the soul is incorruptible, untainted by outside influences. Regression is unlikely during this final stage of alchemy called *fixation* whereby *yin* and *yang*, unconscious and conscious, the right and left hemispheres of the brain work from a state of equilibrium.

The four elements coming together may be the four rivers merging as one in the biblical Garden of Eden. Dream 70 reminded me that Paradise awaits. In fact, I have heard the words 'rebirth to Eden' and been encouraged to continue with environmental healing in my dreams. Collective awakening to higher consciousness may be the means to return to the Golden Age predicted in ancient civilizations such as the Incas and sought after by esoteric organizations such as the Hermetic Order of the Golden Dawn. The cross within the Earth in dream 71 hints at the possibility for peace and goodwill on a planetary level. As the alchemists say, within all physical matter, including ourselves, is the pure potential of spiritual essence.[62] We start by finding peace within the center of our own being. To heal the world, we must first heal ourselves.

Dream 72: I am given homework by an unknown teacher to look up the meaning of the names in the Bible.
Dream 73: I am told the Bible works in metaphor.
Dream 74: Recurring dreams of Mary Magdalene and crystal skulls.

Mary means 'light giver' or 'enlightened', and Magdalen 'unconquered' and 'magnificent'.[31] Mary Magdalen, as an enlightened being, is known by Gnostic Christians as the 'woman who knew the All'.[63] The center of the Egyptian Ourborus also tells us 'All is One!' Being unconquered we represent a state of naturalness. We are the light bearers and through sharing our light with others we create a more peaceful world around us.

Dream 74 suggests that there may be scientific basis behind Qigong and the alchemy of the brain. Research shows that mindfulness meditation helps bring people into the present moment. UCLA researchers found that regular practice has many health benefits. Mindfulness increases activation of the right hemisphere within the prefrontal cortex increasing feelings of oneness. Meditation also has a calming influence on the primary emotional center of the brain, the amygdale.[64] The amygdala is responsible for destructive emotions such as fear, anger and outrage. This part of the brain associates events with emotion, labeling them as good or bad before they get stored as memory. The amygdala brain allows the emotional past to filter our perception and detract from present experience. Through meditation, however, we clear the negative emotional programming of our past; perhaps that is the physical biology behind spiritual enlightenment.

I believe the amygdala is comparable to the *yin* soul. The *yin* soul is responsible for the seven emotions in Chinese Medicine. These negative emotions, considered the internal evils of the body, account for about 85 per cent of disease according to Chinese theory. Qigong movement meditation and other internal cultivation techniques are important as they release emotional attachments (cravings) and avoidance behavior (fears): those challenges that the Buddha overcame to become enlightened under the Bodhi tree. Becoming liberated, an individual can act authentically and spontaneously, freely expressing joyful bliss from a liberated heart. Western doctors link stress to 60 to 90 per cent of doctor visits.[65] By removing the negative associations to events we can calm the stress response. Minimizing our reactions to stressful events, individuals live happier and healthier lives with increased life expectancy and quality of living.

The *po* body soul has symbolic connections to the amygdala emotional center of the brain. The *po* soul is linked to the lungs and the metal element in Chinese Medicine. The lungs are associated with the sensory organ of the nose through which we breathe and smell. How interesting that the emotional center of the brain, the amygdala, is also associated with the function of smell, particularly with sexual arousal.[66]

Mary Magdalene is also symbolically connected to the *po* body soul and the amygdala brain center. The body soul governs the animal instincts such as physical sexuality. Likewise, Mary Magdalene has had a reputation as either a harlot or tantric spiritual adept. She is associated with sexual liberation and may have been the spiritual and intimate partner or wife of Jesus. Like the *po* soul she is associated with the number seven. Mary Magdalene is referred to in the Bible as having seven devils cast out. She symbolically represents the *yin* soul and the alchemical process of removing the unhealthy emotions from the body.

Mary Magdalene and other goddess archetypes teach the importance of purifying negative connotations about healthy sexuality. Getting back into enjoying our physical bodies through movement, we develop a positive body image. As a result we are happier, enjoying constructive emotional bonding with others. By freeing our innate instincts, we take an important step in our spiritual development.

In Christian art, the skull is a symbol often found with images of Mary Magdalene.[2] I have seen this in paintings in cathedrals in Europe and South America and wondered about the significance. The skull within a ring of ivy is a symbol of eternal life.[67] Placing Mary Magdalene as a metaphor for the skull (as well as the amygdala), we have a figure representing the physiological path to immortality. Maybe this is why Magdalene as a representative of body wisdom has been linked with the woman in the World card. She reminds us, above all else, that illumination comes from direct personal experience. Through body-minded practices we can bring forth what is within us, returning to our true selves. As Jesus mentions in the Gospel of Thomas it is the way to being saved. The alternative of hiding from our innate nature is destructive. Jesus' message sounds very Taoist to me but then 'the Way' home IS bigger than any one philosophy or religion.

We find the woman figure in the World card dancing freely and effortlessly. With only a spiral around her body, she is pure and natural self expression. Within the whirling emptiness of central *qi,* she lives in the eternal Tao. Holding a double terminated crystal in each hand, the woman shows a balance of left and right hemispheres and heaven and earth within. Living in harmonious awareness, she dances as Spirit moves her. Through sublime movements, she participates in the dance of creation of the world soul, sharing her light and blessings with others. She is the inner being of the Fool and the liberated soul of anyone and everyone, including you.

The fluid movements of a dancer are captured in this statue from the Anatolia Museum in Turkey.

Dream 75: My dad had been a hostage over six weeks and I was exhausted and losing hope. Contact with his captives had dwindled and there were no new leads. The emotional and physical hardship was lowering my spirits so I went to pray in my room. Alone on my bed with eyes closed, I called upon God. I saw dark clouds begin to roll in the sky in my mind's eye. I was beginning to resist and fight

> *this image; then I stopped myself. I was so deep down to my bones tired I didn't want to deny my inner experience anymore and I surrendered to the uncomfortable feelings and images. Without thought to outcome, I was in pure being. Suddenly, I was aware that the energy had shifted and the clouds lightened, creating a circle. Where the clouds parted, the central image of the sun appeared shining its golden rays bright and strong.*

I did not know the significance of what had happened in the prayerful meditation, but it felt like something very powerful had just occurred in the inner realm of my dreaming, in a temporary state of nonbeing. Several hours later, the phone rang and I woke up, racing out of habit to answer the phone in case there was any word about my dad. My primary contact from the Australian Government was on the other end of the phone. With a new found lightness in his voice, he told me my dad had been rescued by Iraqi troops just hours earlier after an unexpected tip off by a local Iraqi civilian. It took a while for the good news to sink in and to realize that my dad was once again safe. The horror of the past six and a half weeks was now over.

People tell me that I was helpful in the release of my dad. All the work writing letters, working on international blogs, helping prepare press releases, finding pictures and medical histories, government planning and family strategizing or peace-keeping were nothing compared to that one small act of spiritual surrender. I feel deeply that our biggest potential is in nondoing rather than doing busy work. We can accomplish so much working through the Dreamtime without any effort. If we all gave our issues and concerns up to a higher power (whether

> Legend tells that the magic circular hollow opening (ouroborus) of the Wishing Tree near Melbourne, Australia helped a father find his missing son around the year 1900 CE.

God, Tao, or our higher selves), just IMAGINE what we could achieve.

About four weeks into my dad's hostage situation, I recall walking my dog and hearing and feeling in the wind that everything would be fine. I went through my own personal crisis and wondered if I trusted the dreams and intuition that appeared to contrast my physical reality. My extended family was preparing for a possible funeral and the situation seemed bleak. But if I couldn't believe in myself and my own internal guidance system, what could I believe and trust in? It was a deep soul searching moment for me and a test of faith that I ultimately passed.

How do miracles work? It is the great mystery of life...

Dream 76: During Qigong, I feel myself as the Greek messenger god Hermes. I feel the presence of numerous dream guides including the Native American woman and man from my vision almost ten years ago. I feel their presence and an air of expectation for an upcoming joyful celebration. That night as I fall asleep, I feel myself ascend and become one with the wind. Letting go of personal awareness I move in an etheric dance with the totality of the universe - complete, whole and so much bigger than my habitual concept of myself.

Dream 77: During my morning dreaming I am surprised to hear my voice say, 'I am God.'

In the Acts of John, Jesus said, 'To the universe belongs the dancer. He who does not dance does not know what happens'.[68] The *ab* is the Egyptian word for the heart soul, the most important of the seven souls. The hieroglyph for *ab* is a dancing figure. It represents the mystical dance of the heart.[69] In India, the heart beat of the cosmos and the balance of immanent and transcendent is depicted by the fiery dance of Shiva. Fire again is the element of the heart.

This spiritual journey through the Tao of Tarot began consciously almost ten years earlier when I realized the difference between who I was inside and what I had become. At that point, I dreamed of the Native American woman billowing upwards in the wind and transforming into an angel of light. To reach my goal of authentic and joyful living, I was, as the Native American man showed me, to open my heart and allow the transcendent to flow through me. Dreaming would be my guide and lead me to Qigong and a transformational process of spiritual unfolding that surpassed my wildest expectations. A decade later I feel back on track and am enjoying the fluidity and ease of the magical and fulfilling existence of my synchronistic life.

Reddish clay sculpture of the Hindu god Shiva dancing within the eternal flame.

As I write this, two months short of those ten years (I was asked to submit this manuscript to O Books Publishing ten years to the day), I feel I have experienced the divination process of the tarot and come to glimpse the 'I Am' presence of God within. The Native American woman has told me that her name is Rainbow Dancing Heart. She is, as are all dream figures, a depiction of myself as well as the woman in the World card. Gazing upon her image in the Waite tarot, I feel her smiling eyes reflecting back upon me.

I celebrate the completeness of this chapter in my life and hope that others will be inspired to pursue Qigong Dreaming and join me in the collective dance of the cosmos. I am extremely grateful for all that I have been able to release and all the gifts and opportunities that have come as a result. Spiritual practice is about self discover and letting go of our separation from God. Clearing away the self imposed road blocks, everything else falls into place including physical, emotional and spiritual well being. Following the intuitive center of the heart we cannot but find the elusive elixir of immortality and the path back to the Garden of Paradise. Being like the Fool we trust in the infinite intelligence behind life and enjoy without expectation wherever the next step of the journey takes us.

My love wanders the rooms, melodious,
Flute notes, plucked wires,
Full of a wine the Magi drank
On the way to Bethlehem
We are three, the moon comes
From its quiet corner, puts a pitcher of water
Down in the center. The circle
Of surface flames.
One of us kneels to kiss the threshold.
One drinks, with wine flames playing over his face.
One watches the gathering,
And says to any cold onlookers,
This dance is the joy of existence.

Rumi poem #2395
Translated by Coleman Barks

Appendix I: Bibliography

1. *Voyager Tarot,* James Wanless, Knutson, 1984
2. *The Woman's Dictionary of Symbols and Sacred Objects,* Barbara G. Walker, Harpers & Row, 1988
3. *Alchemy & Alchemists,* Sean Martin, Chartwell Books, Inc, 2006
4. *The Merriam-Webster Dictionary,* Merriam-Webster, 2004
5. *The Return of the Serpents of Wisdom,* Mark Amaru Pinkham, Adventures Unlimited Press, 1997
6. *The Art of Internal Observation and Panoramic Knowing: Laozi's Classic on the Way of Virtues,* Guan Cheng Sun, Ph.D. & Jill Gonet M.F.A, Qi: The Journal of Traditional Eastern Health & Fitness Vol 18, No. 1, Spring 2008
7. *Vital Breath of the Dao: Chinese Shamanic Tiger Qigong,* Laohu Gong, Master Zhongxian Wu, Dragon Door Publications, 2006
8. *Everything You Need to Know to Feel Go(o)d,* Candice B. Pert, Ph.D., Hay House, Inc. 2006
9. *Mysteries of the Unknown: Secrets of the Alchemists,* edited by George Constable, Time Life Books, 1990
10. *Shiva: The Wild God of Power & Ecstasy,* Wolf Dieter Storl, Inner Traditions, 2004
11. *The Book of Imaginary Beings,* Jorge Luis Borges, Viking Penguin Group, 2005
12. *Nourishing Destiny: The Inner Tradition of Chinese Medicine,* Lonny S. Jarrett, Spirit Path Press, 2004
13. *The Woman's Encyclopedia of Myths and Secrets,* Barbara G. Walker, Harper, 1983
14. *The Foundations of Chinese Medicine,* Giovanni Maciocia, Churchill Livingstone, 2005
15. Shiatsu for Midwives training by Suzanne Yates in Portland, OR 13 September 2006
16. *Welcome to Aboriginal land Uluru Kata Tjuta National Park Visitor Guide and Maps,* Australian Government Director of

National Parks, August 2007

17. *Guardians of the Holy Grail: The Knights Templar, John the Baptist and the Waters of Life*, Mark Amaru Pinkham, Adventures Unlimited Press, 2004

18. *The Cult of the Black Virgin*, Ean Begg, ARKANA Penguin Books, 1996

19. *Five Element Constitutional Acupuncture*, Angela Hicks, John Hicks & Peter Mole, Churchill Livingstone, 2004

20. *A History of Religious Ideas, Volume 2, From Gautama Buddha to the Triumph of Christianity*, Mircea Eliade, The University of Chicago Press, 1982

21. Soaring Crane Qigong Training by Teri Applegate, passing information from Professor Hui Xian Chen at The Oregon College of Oriental Medicine, 2001

22. *Transcendence and Divine Passion: The Queen Mother of the West in Medieval China*, Suzanne Cahill, Stanford University Press, 1993

23. *Thicker Than Water: the Origins of Blood as Symbol and Ritual*, Melissa L. Meyer, Routledge Taylor & Francis Group, 2005

24. *Chinese Medical Qigong Therapy Volume 5: An Energetic Approach to Oncology*, Alan Johnson Ph.D. DTCM, DMQ (China), The International Institute of Medical Qigong, 2005

25. Interview with Richard F. Bryant, Geomancer, Vastu & Feng Shui practitioner WA USA

26. *Chinese Medical Qigong Therapy: A Comprehensive Clinical Text*, Alan Johnson Ph.D., D.T.C.M., D.M.Q. (China), The International Institute of Medical Qigong, 2000

27. *A History of Religious Ideas, Volume 1, From the Stone Age to the Eleusinian Mysteries*, Mircea Eliade translation William R. Trask, The University of Chicago Press, 1978

28. *Transformation of Myth Through Time*, Joseph Campbell Harper & Row Publishers, 1990

29. *The Shining Ones: The World's Most Powerful Secret Society Revealed*, Philip Gardiner & Gary Osborn, Watkins Publishing,

2006

30. *Sagas of the Norsemen: Viking and German Myth,* Duncan Baird Publishers, Duncan Baird Publishers, 1997

31. *Mary Magdalene: The Illuminator Adventures,* William Henry, Unlimited Press, 2006

32. *The Underworld in Myth, Magic and Mystery,* Sydney Baggs Ph.D. & Joan Baggs, Bowker's Books, 2003

33. *When the Drummers Were Women,* Layne Redmond, Three Rivers Press & Random House, 1997

34. *Gods of the Egyptians 2 vols.* Sir E. A. Wallis Budge, Dover, 1969

35. *Secrets of Ancient and Sacred Places: The World's Mysterious Heritage,* Paul Devereux, Brockhampton Press, 1992

36. *Kundalini: The Arousal of the Inner Energy,* Ajit Mookerjee, Destiny Books, 1986

37. *Mother Daughter Wisdom: Understanding the Crucial Link Between Mothers, Daughters, and Health,* Christiane Northrup, M.D., Bantam Books, 2005

38. *The Land of Osiris: An Introduction to Khemitology,* Stephen S. Mehler, The Adventures Unlimited Press, 2001

39. *Chinese Characters,* L. Weiger, Paragon Book Reprint, 1965

40. *100 Wonders of the World: From Manmade Masterpieces to Breathtaking Surprises of Nature,* Michael Hoffman & Alexander Krings, Parragon Publishing, 2007

41. *The Tower of Alchemy: An Advanced Guide to the Great Work,* Henry Goddard, Red Wheel Weiser, 1999

42. *Holy Blood, Holy Grail: The Secret History of Jesus, The Shocking Legacy of the Grail,* Michael Baigent, Richard Leigh & Henry Lincoln, Bantam Doubleday Dell Publishing Group, 2005

43. *Jesus the Magician,* Morton Smith, Harper & Row, 1978

44. *Mary Magdalene, Bride in Exile,* Margaret Starbird, Bear & Company, 2005

45. *The Zelator: The Secret Journals of Mark Hedsel,* David Ovason, Arrow, 1999 referenced from the Illustrated World Encyclopedia Bobley Publishing Corp.

46. *The Inner Reaches of Outer Space: Metaphor as Myth and As Religion,* Joseph Campbell, Perennial Library Harper & Row, 1986

47. *My Stroke of Insight: A Brain Scientist's Personal Journey,* Jill Bolte Taylor, Ph.D., Viking & Penguin Group, 2006

48. *The Book of Balance and Harmony,* T. Cleary, North Point Press, 1989

49. Teachings by The Mystic Christ Celine who resides in Ashland, Oregon USA.

50. *Dreambody: The Body's Role in Revealing the Self,* Arnold Mindell, Lao Tse Press, 1998

51. *Voices of the First Day: Awakening in the Aboriginal Dreamtime,* R. Lawlor,. Inner Traditions, 1991

52. *Sophia: The Gnostic Archetype of Feminine Soul Wisdom,* Stephan Hoeller from the book *The Goddess Re Awakening: The Feminine Principle Today,* Shirley Nicholson, Theosopical Publishing House, 1989

53. *Pedigree: the Origin of Words From Nature,* Stephen Potter & Laurens Sargent, Taplinger Publishing Co.,1974

54. *Amulets and Talismans,* Sir E.A. Wallis Budge, University Books Inc., 1968

55. *Dictionary of the Tarot,* Bill Butles, Schocken Books, 1975

56. *The Teachings of the Essenes From Enoch to the Dead Sea Scrolls,* Edmond Bordeaux Szekely & Walden Saffron, The C.W. Daniel Company Limited, Church Path, 1978

57. *The Mysterious, Magickal Cat,* D. J. Conway, Llewellyn Publications, 1998

58. *Clinical Dialysis, Allen R. Nissenson, Richard N. Fine,* McGraw Hill Professional, 2005

59. *Rumi: We Are Three Translator,* Coleman Barks, Maypop Books, 1987

60. *Jung and Tarot: An Archetypal Journey,* Sally Nichols Weiser Books, 1980

61. *An Instinct for Dragons,* David E. Jones, Routledge, 2002

62. *The Weiser Concise Guide to Alchemy*, Brian Cotnoir, Weiser Books, 2006

63. *Mary Magdalene: Myth and Metaphor*, Susan Haskins, Harcourt Brace, 1994

64. *The Science of Mindfulness Meditation*, John M. Grohol, Psy.D., Psych Central, June 25, 2007. Los Angeles, CA

65. *Brain Check*, H. Benson, M.D., J. Corliss & G. Cowley, Newsweek September 24, 2004

66. *The Limbic System Connections: Teaching and the Human Brain*, Renate Nummela Caine & Geoffrey Caine, Making_Incentive Publications, 1990

67. *Dictionary of Subjects and Symbols in Art*, James Hall, Harper & Row, 1974

68. *The Gnostic Gospels*, Elaine Pagels, Random House, 1979

69. *Egyptian Language*, Sir E. A.Wallis Budge, Dover Publications, 1977

Appendix II: Glossary of Qigong Terms

Bai Hui: Known as Hundred Meeting Point. This acupoint is at the apex of the body. It is the highest point along the Governing Vessel called GV-20. It is often used in Qigong to bring the energy of heaven into the body.

Chong Qi: Transformative central life force energy formed when yin and yang principles unite as one. The movement of central *qi* is compared to a void or whirling emptiness that leads one back to the Tao.

Chong Mai: The most important energy meridian for body-mind-spirit health in the body according to Chinese Medicine. This energy channel runs through the center of the head and body linking the three internal treasures called *dan tian*. A focus in Qigong, it is where heaven and earth unite in the body.

Dai Mai: Known as the Belt or Girdle Channel this energy channel flows horizontally around the waist regulating the vertical flow of energy of the other major meridians.

Dan Tian: Translates as elixir field or cinnabar field. These lower, middle and upper energy reservoirs exist in the lower abdomen, the center of the chest and the center of the head respectively.

Dao De Jing: The Taoist Classic attributed to Lao Tzu showing 'the Way' to authentic living, health, happiness and spiritual wisdom.

De: The virtues that arise from being in harmony with the Tao. These include moral character and the qualities of kindness, compassion and benevolence.

Du Mai: Also known as the Governing Vessel (GV) and the Root of all Yang, this important energy channel flows along the spine. It is the upwards aspect of the microcosmic orbit.

Feng Shui: Translates as Wind Water. It is a means to restore harmony and abundance in the environment through balance of the five elements.

Fu Xi: Depicted as half dragon, half man he was the male and masculine aspect of the original couple. He was attributed with creating the I Ching and bringing agriculture and the sciences to humankind.

Guanjie: The joints of the body. The joints are believed to act as energetic gates allowing spiritual energy into the body.

Hui Yin: Translates as Meeting of Yin and Metal Gate. This important acupoint is the first point on the Conception Vessel or CV-1. It is located between the legs on the perineum floor between the sexual organ and the anus. By opening this point one nourishes the Governing Vessel, Conception Vessel and Central Channel.

Hun: The masculine aspect of the soul called the evolutionary soul. This aspect of the soul is related to the element of wood and the direction of the East.

I Ching: The Book of Changes is a book of wisdom describing the cyclical nature of life and the way to harmonious living.

Jing: Physical essence, the sexual/creative energy of the body stored in the lower *dan tian.*

Lao Gong: Acupoint located in the center of the palms. This acupoint is commonly used in Qigong practice to guide the energy in the body and for external healing.

Lao Tzu: Legendary founder of Taoism thought to have authored the Taoist Classic Tao de Jing.

Ling: The feminine aspect of Spirit relating to spiritual potency.

Mai: The rhythmic pulsation from the heart contraction as well as the overall circulatory system of the blood.

Nu Wa: The half dragon, half woman divine being who was the feminine aspect of the original couple. She is the Creatrix who in legend made people from clay and weaved the stars in the sky.

Po: The feminine aspect of the soul called the corporeal or body soul. This aspect of the soul is relating to the element of metal and the direction of the West.

Qi: Life force energy flowing within our bodies and everything in the universe. The healthy flow of vital energy within the energy channels nourishes the cells of the body and leads to holistic wellness.

Qigong: Translates as working with life force energy. It is a body oriented cultivation technique and gentle movement exercise for physical, emotional and spiritual wellbeing. This practice is based on the energy system of Chinese Medicine.

Ren Mai: Known as the Conception Vessel (CV) and the Root of all Yin. This important energy pathway runs along the front midline of the body. It is the downward aspect of the microcosmic orbit.

Shen: The masculine aspect of Spirit related to consciousness and mental thought.

Taiji: Represents unity through interrelationship of feminine (yin) and masculine (yang) forces in nature.

Tian Mu: Extra point called Heavenly Collector between the eyebrows in the center of the forehead. This point is an external link to the upper *dan tian.*

Wu: Lao Tzu teaches that emptiness (of the intellect) is the first step to finding the Way.

Wu: A word for shaman, healer, rainmakers, medium and soul travelers of ancient China. They were able to travel into different dimensions of reality in the dream state.

Xian: A spiritual immortal; one who is transcendent, superhuman and a celestial being.

Xiwangmu: Queen of the West, Taoist goddess of life and immortality who sits upon Kunlun Mountain in the Paradise of the West and guides worthy individuals to immortality. First reference predates Taoism in the Shang Dynasty (1766 to 1122 BCE).

Xuan: The doorway to the golden secret of all life when emptiness (wu) and inner awareness (you) are maintained. Comparable to the gateway to the unconscious and the aboriginal Dreamtime.

Yin: Comparable to the dark side of the mountain and associated with the qualities of cool, deep, quiet, moist, internal and low in the body and found in Nature.

You: Inner awareness through dreams and intuition leads to the appearance of the infinite intelligence of the Tao.

Yang: Comparable to the bright side of the mountain and associated with the qualities of warm, superficial, excited, dry, external and high in the body and in Nature.

Appendix III

Description of how to do Spiral Qigong

Bring the tip of your tongue upwards to connect with the upper palate just behind the front upper teeth. Bring a smile from your heart to your eyes and out to the universe. Relax the focus of your gaze, slowly closing your eyes and bringing in your spiritual light. Relax the body part by part. Working downward from the top of the head, let go of any tensions and tightness held there by gently bringing the mind's attention to each successive area. Spend a few moments connecting with the energy of the head, neck, shoulders, upper arms, elbows, forearms, wrists, hands, fingers, chest, waist, lower abdomen, upper back, middle back, lower back, pelvic girdle, thighs, knees, legs, ankles, feet and toes. Prime and loosen the joints by letting them begin to move and express themselves. Focus on allowing the head, shoulders, wrists and elbows, the hips, ankles and the whole spine to let go and move on their own for a few minutes. Now, visualize yourself in a beautiful place in nature filled with wondrous *qi*. Allow the scenery details to present themselves and change, knowing they are being directed by your higher self. When you are ready to begin, bring your mind's attention to the center of your palms, the acupoint known as *Lao Gong*. Turn your palms forward and imagine yourself holding a ball of vibrant energy or *qi* in front of your body. Holding this ball of swirling energy, you may have a sense of its pure vibration and harmonious perfection as you tune into and sense it. While focusing on the palms of your hands and with relaxed arms and hands, use your shoulders to slowly lift the ball of *qi* upward towards the heavens allowing it to absorb the energies of the stars, the moon, the sun and the celestial bodies of the heavens. When your hands reach the level of your ears, relax your wrists turning palms downward. Bending your elbows to the sides, slowly and naturally guide the ball of *qi* down through *Bai Hui* at the top of the head and into the central pillar of the Central Channel. Moving your hands softly downward in front of the body, feel or imagine the energy going through the middle of the head, through the center of the chest and into the lower *dan tian* at the center of the lower abdomen. Continue to guide the *qi* downward from the lower abdomen, down through *Hui Yin* between the legs. Arms extend downwards and straighten as you continue to direct the *qi* with your mind's eye into the ground, between your feet and downward through the layers of the earth. Feel or imagine the energy entering the center or heart of the earth and gently rest your attention there. Keeping your mind's eye deep within the earth, feel or imagine the energies blending, churning and swirling. Allow the potential energy to build until the energies shift and begin spiraling upwards in a counterclockwise direction around the body. Allow the central *qi* to whirl and blend with the energies of your body. Do not try to direct the flow of energy to any particular location, just allow it to guide your whole being. Begin to move and express your body consciousness through movement.

When you are ready to conclude, slow down your movements until your body comes to a rest. Gently place both hands on the lower abdomen. The left hand goes on top for women and the right hand on top for men for the perfect *yin yang* balance. With eyes still closed, take a few deep breaths grounding the energies you have generated, the fruits of your Qigong practice, deeply into your lower *dan tian*. When you feel the energy is stable and condensed into a small sphere within the center of the pelvic girdle, slowly open your eyes.

Be thankful for this time to reconnect with yourself through Qigong. Intend to carry the benefits of Qigong practice in the days and weeks ahead, letting your authentic nature shine.

Cautionary Note: In this spontaneous Qigong form, it is important to allow the energies to flow naturally and to not let the limited ego mind run the show. Forcing energies to move up the spine or intentionally contracting *Hui Yin*, for example, may not be in your best interest and could cause negative effects such as overriding the bioelectrical system of the body. Listen and recognize when your body has had enough. It may be only a few minutes or a few seconds but the practice is potent nonetheless. Stop and rest if uncomfortable symptoms such as dizziness, headache or nausea arise. Note that the body could need time to assimilate higher frequencies of energy coming in.

If feelings of discomfort present themselves afterwards, the symptoms may reflect a healing crisis showing where long term issues or emotions have been stuck and stored internally. Symptoms may be coming into conscious awareness and therefore experienced for the first time. However, always check with a doctor if there are any symptoms of concern. If symptoms are sub clinical, not reflective of a health issue, Qigong students can consider additional energy modalities such as acupuncture, herbal medicine, shiatsu Japanese bodywork, homeopathy, cranio sacral therapy, reflexology, massage, homeopathy and Reiki in addition to Qigong practice to facilitate the clearing of the issue at hand.

O is a symbol of the world, of oneness and unity. In different cultures it also means the "eye," symbolizing knowledge and insight. We aim to publish books that are accessible, constructive and that challenge accepted opinion, both that of academia and the "moral majority."

Our books are available in all good English language bookstores worldwide. If you don't see the book on the shelves ask the bookstore to order it for you, quoting the ISBN number and title. Alternatively you can order online (all major online retail sites carry our titles) or contact the distributor in the relevant country, listed on the copyright page.

See our website **www.o-books.net** for a full list of over 500 titles, growing by 100 a year.

And tune in to myspiritradio.com for our book review radio show, hosted by June-Elleni Laine, where you can listen to the authors discussing their books.